If Only

If Only

DAVID A. SEAMANDS

V/ VICTOR BOOKS
A DIVISION OF SCRIPTURE PRESS PUBLICATIONS INC.
USA CANADA ENGLAND

Editors: Carole Streeter and Barbara Williams

Designer: Andrea Boven
Cover Photo: Tony Stone Images

To the newer members of the Seamands cast,
our grandchildren in order of their appearance.

David
Matthew
Jason
Joseph
Sarah
Stephanie
Daniel
Joel
Hannah

Acknowledgments

I want to express deepest appreciation to my loving wife, Helen, for her patient assistance as my Living Voice Computer. Her built-in software (soft-wear) includes a dictionary, grammar, thesaurus, and hymnal. I just shout from my office, "Honey, how do you spell asspearagus?" or "Does that word have a hyphen in it?" or "Do you remember the stanza in one of Charles Wesley's hymns which says something about a 'spring'?" And quicker than I can say *Microsoft Word*, she calls back with the right answer! She is still the best gift God ever gave me.

I also want to thank Carole Streeter, whom God sent along fifteen years ago to push me into writing. She continues to assist me in editing, proofing, and shaping the general concepts of my books. Once again, her help has been invaluable.

David A. Seamands
Nokomis, Florida
1995

Contents

1   The Great Blame Game 13

2   The Mystery of Love versus Suffering . . . 29

3   Moving into the Present 43

4   The Ultimate Victim 57

5   Letting in the Light 71

6   Looking into the Grave 85

7   Shadows in the Darkness 101

8   The Ifs of Belief 121

9   Group Grace 143

10   Joseph — No If Onlys 161

     Notes 179

"The woman You put here . . .
she gave me . . . and I ate it. . . ."

"The serpent deceived me,
and I ate."

Genesis 3:12-13

1

The Great
Blame Game

As I look back over almost fifty years of Christian service, I realize that I have spent a lifetime ministering to broken and hurting people. Through preaching, pastoral counseling, and writing, I have tried to help people understand the close connection between their wounds and scars from the past and their spiritual defeats and failures of the present. In my early years this emphasis was much needed, particularly among evangelicals. For we gave the impression that any emotional problem was the direct result of some sin we had deliberately chosen, and for which we were personally responsible. The fact that some people were the victims of others who had sinned against them was quite underemphasized, if not totally ignored. The idea that sympathetic understanding, counseling, and a deeper level of prayer was necessary for their healing, sometimes even for their salvation, tended to be badly neglected. Everything was considered to be a purely spiritual problem with a purely spiritual answer.

I have long been concerned with this imbalance, and through my preaching, counseling, and writing have worked to correct it by ministering to damaged, dysfunctional, and despairing people. My aim was to lead them to know Christ as their Savior, Healer, and Wonderful Counselor who could bring them to emotional, spiritual, and relational wholeness. In that sense I have spent my life ministering to victims.

However, I now have a new concern. Have we evangelicals moved too far in the other direction? Are we in danger of losing our balance and going to the opposite extreme? In the May 17, 1993 issue of *Christianity Today*, "The Therapeutic Revolution" addressed this fear as several leaders in the movement shared this same concern.

I am personally most alarmed by the possibility that evangelical Christian counseling may itself become a victim! A victim to what has become a national epidemic—the obsession with *victimism* or *victimology*. This is the Great Blame Game in which people try to escape personal responsibility for their choices and excuse almost any kind of behavior by finding somebody else to blame.

Unfortunately, the epidemic has infected many individual Christian counselees. Instead of using the insights discovered through counseling as a means of grace and sanctification, the process of growing more Christlike, some counselees seem to be using them as a means of escaping personal responsibility and excusing lower standards of Christian living.

These are some of the concerns that finally pressed me into an in-depth study which resulted in the birthing of this book. As I discovered what Scripture had to say on the subject of responsibility and healing, I was struck by an amazing paradox—there were all kinds of victims described in its pages but no victimization! That is, plenty of victims—suffering people who had no choice in, control over, or responsibility for what happened to them. But there was no victimhood—people who were allowed to claim victimization as the reason for *who* and *what* they were, and *how* they were living out their lives. I then felt guided to base my study on the key words in the whole issue—"If" and "If Only."

If or If Only?

Many people consider the word "If" to be the weakest word in the Bible and the English language. This is the "If" which always looks backward with complaint, regret, or blame, and is

used as an excuse not only for handicaps but also for sins and
failures. As a pastoral counselor, I have heard people use the
word constantly. They usually emphasize its hopelessness and
futility by turning it into the common phrase, "If only."

Then one day it dawned on me that "If" is also the strongest
word, when it is the forward-looking "If" of faith. This faith
that believes in God's promises is the only condition for receiving their fulfillment. While the weak, backward-looking "If
only" is a cop-out from responsibility, the strong, believing "If"
is a plug-in to reservoirs of God's power.

I want us to look at several of these biblical "Ifs" as they
occur in both a positive and negative sense. In order to clarify
the distinctions between these two uses of the word, I will
sometimes paraphrase an "If" in the text of Scripture with an
"If only" when it obviously conveys that meaning.

The weak and strong "Ifs" stand in sharpest contrast in the
familiar story of the raising of Lazarus in John 11. Martha and
Mary's complaint in verses 11 and 32, "Lord, if only You had
been here, my brother would not have died," are in vivid
contrast to Jesus' challenge in verse 40, "Did I not tell you that
if you believed, you would see the glory of God?"

The Lazarus story will form the basic outline and set the
tone for most of the book, for in its details are many of the
biblical concepts so relevant to this subject. It also contains
some of the most important theological questions and spiritual
issues involved in Christian counseling, healing, and the entire
process of being restored to wholeness in Christ. As we come
to understand it more deeply, I trust we will all identify ourselves as a part of that original group in Bethany.

A National Epidemic

Some years ago comedian Flip Wilson's famous line, "The
devil made me do it," was always good for a laugh. We recognized it as a common line we had all used — one of those
standard human excuses to escape responsibility for our sins
and failures. Laughter was actually a healthy response. We

laughed because we realized it was too funny to be true. We knew that whatever may have put the temptation in our minds, the choice was ours, and we couldn't blame anything or anyone—no, not even the devil.

Now it's different. A stand-up comedian summarized the three phases of American history this way: First, the passing of the buffalo; second, the passing of the Indian; and third, the passing of the buck. He illustrated the third phase by referring to a recent cartoon picturing a courtroom scene. A black-robed judge seated behind his desk is questioning the defendant before him, "How do you wish to plead? Guilty? Not guilty? Not guilty by reason of insanity? Not guilty by reason of hypoglycemic sugar reaction? Not guilty by reason of caffeine, nicotine, or drug withdrawal? Or, not guilty by reason of inadequate parenting?" Though we may laugh, now our laughter is more nervous and hesitant. We realize we've got a serious problem on our hands. This time it's too true to be funny.

The "If only," "Don't blame me," and "It's not my fault" attitudes are symptoms of a serious national epidemic— "victimology." Even the secular press is alarmed about the rapid spread of "victimization" or "victimism." In 1991, *New York* magazine had a cover story on "The New Culture of Victimization," with the headline "Don't Blame Me!" *Harpers* entitled their feature, "Victims All?" and *Time* magazine's cover story was, "Crybabies: Eternal Victims." As for television, in the last few years not only the sensational talk shows but also the serious investigative news programs like "Now," "Forty-Eight Hours," "Dateline," "Sixty Minutes," "Prime Time," "20/20," and others have done segments on what has come to be known as "The Blame Game." We have seen dramatizations of the amazing and sometimes bizarre lengths to which individuals have gone. Civil and criminal lawsuits range from the ludicrous to the dangerous.

In Pennsylvania a school district employee, fired for always being late to work, sued his employer. His lawyer argued he was a victim of "chronic lateness syndrome."

In the tiny village of Savona, New York, a thirteen-year-old enticed a four-year-old boy into the woods and sexually abused him before bludgeoning him to death. Although the jury did not accept it, the defense seriously contended he could not be blamed, since he had come from a dysfunctional home, had suffered from low self-esteem resulting from the taunts of other children about his strange-looking ears, and was the victim of a "rage disorder, an intermittent, explosive mental disorder."

Perhaps the most publicized case was that of the Menendez brothers, Eric and Lyle. One night in 1989 they brutally murdered their parents, called 911 for help, and then blamed it on an unknown Mafia hitman. Eric even gave an emotional eulogy at the funeral. They then took the $14 million they had inherited and went on a near million-dollar spending spree.

Months later their confession, taped for a psychologist, was made public. In it they admitted to the ghastly cold-bloodedness of the murders. A large part of the Menendez's fortune was spent on the best defense lawyers. But how could they persuade a jury to "understand" the savagery of the killings — sixteen rounds of ammunition at close range? There was only one way: turn the villains into victims who had suffered terrible and painful sexual abuse at the hands of their father. The entire nation was shocked at the incredible travesty of justice when they were acquitted as a result of hung juries.

An even more recent case involved Colin Ferguson, who grew up in an affluent Jamaican home, immigrated to the USA and lived in New York City. In December 1993, he went to California, waited the required fifteen days for buying a gun, returned home, and boarded the Long Island subway at the evening rush hour. Then in a carefully planned shooting spree, he killed six people and wounded nineteen others. His pockets were found to be filled with racial hate notes. On NBC's "NOW," his lawyer stated that while he felt sorry for the victims and their families, Ferguson was the *real victim* — a victim of the "black rage syndrome" which had "pushed him over the edge."

Alan Dershowitz, one of the country's best known defense lawyers who has been involved in getting several famous clients "off the hook," was interviewed on the Charlie Rose show. As one of O.J. Simpson's attorneys, he has been completely open about their strategy. "Now you are going to see the defense brutally attacking these victims. By the end of the trial, nobody's going to have a kind thing to say about the two dead people." This is why I was shocked to hear him in a later interview on "Good Morning America," talking about his new book, *The Abuse Excuse*. He expressed concern regarding the many cases where "tragic histories have been used as an excuse for violent behavior," and described one in which the offender was said to be a victim of "The Holocaust Survivor Syndrome." He stated that judges must put a stop to this sort of thing or our whole judicial system will break down. Could it be that even those who have helped create the Victimology Frankensteins are finally realizing that someday they too may become one of its victims?[1]

Charles J. Sykes, senior fellow at the Wisconsin Policy Research Institute, has written a serious and scholarly study of this in his book, *A Nation of Victims: The Decay of the American Character*. With careful documentation and analysis he shows that the growing national motto, "I am not responsible, it's not my fault because I'm a victim," threatens to destroy the very fabric of society. It now undermines some of the most important foundations of our nation like our systems of education and justice.[2]

A Mental Disorder for Every Occasion

Another evidence of the victimology epidemic is the extremes to which secular psychology and psychiatry have gone. The *Diagnostic and Statistical Manual of Mental Disorders* (DSM) is the nearest equivalent to a Bible for those in the field. From a purely practical standpoint, the DSM has become increasingly important because counselors consult it to decide which code number to use for billing health insurance companies. As a Christian counselor who believes in integrating "truth" from every source, I have sometimes found the DSM helpful in understanding the complexities of the human personality. There are occasions when sin, sickness, and damaged emotions become so intertwined that healing requires the best knowledge humans have discovered along with the highest wisdom God has disclosed in Scripture. The final authority, of course, is God's Word, and all human wisdom must be filtered through it and judged by it.

The latest edition, *DSM-IV*, includes over 300 so-called "mental disorders." That's more than three times the number listed in the 1952 edition. From a biblical standpoint, I feel I must strongly object to some of the conditions described in it, because they are an attempt to explain away personal responsibility for sinful behavior. Such refusal of responsibility violates the moral orderliness which God has built into us, undermines character, and creates even greater emotional and spiritual distress. It spreads the victimization disease and, therefore, worsens rather than heals mental health.

In the *DSM-IV*, I am amazed at what "mental disorders" are now included, everything from "Nicotine Dependence" suffered by smokers, to the "Disorder of Written Expression" which afflicts people who cannot write well. If you've always had trouble with math, then you may be a victim of "Mathematics Disorder" (315.1). Do your children argue with you all the time? Often lose their tempers? Refuse to obey your rules and regulations? Deliberately do things to annoy people? Blame others for their misbehavior, become resentful and act spiteful or vengeful? If they have shown four or more of these "symptoms" during the last six months, they may be suffering from "Oppositional Defiant Disorder" (313.81)!

In fairness, I must say that the *DSM* contains many cautions about using it as a kind of psychological repair manual or recipe book, and warns about the difficulty of judging between what is "normal" and "abnormal." The problem is that the whole mind-set of the book makes it almost impossible to decide just what is "normal." For, believe it or not, there is even a category for those times when nothing seems to fit, Code 300.9: "Unspecified Mental Disorder (nonpsychotic)."[5] Is it any wonder that there is a widespread lack of confidence in the court testimonies from psychological "experts" and the feeling that they have become a part of the Great Blame Game?

Even in the Villages of India

I have spent much of my life listening to the words "If only" in one form or another. Long before I became a pastoral counselor, I heard them during my missionary years (1946–1962) as anevangelist in the villages of India. Our work was largely among people on the lowest rung of the Hindu social and economic ladder—the so-called Outcastes or Untouchables. Modern India has made progress in eradicating many of the evils of the caste system, but in those days the condition of these despised and oppressed people was dreadful. For millenniums they were truly victims of a cruel system made all the more ruthless because it was religious—their karma or state in life was a divinely prescribed victimization. "If only," they would mournfully intone, "we had been born of high caste parents. If only we owned just a small piece of land. If only we didn't have to live in the segregated section of town. If only we could read and write." You can imagine how revolutionary the Good News was to them, and how eagerly they responded to its message of hope.

Although I offered them improvements in education, health, and vocational and agricultural skills, there was something far more important. If these victims were to become victorious over their seemingly hopeless situation, a fundamental inner transformation of spirit had to take place, to turn them from futility to faith. One day while I was baptizing a large group of new Christians, the familiar passage of Scripture which I had memorized as a teenager literally exploded with bright new meaning:

But you are a chosen people, a royal priesthood, a holy nation, a people belonging to God, that you may declare the praises of Him who called you out of darkness into His wonderful light.

Once you were not a people, but now you are the people of God;
once you had not received mercy, but now you have received
mercy (1 Peter 2:9-10, emphasis mine).

I learned that God could change nobodies into somebodies if
only they would give up their "If onlys!" Although I was completely unaware of it at the time, this was a deeply significant
discovery through which God was teaching me some important
truths regarding the place of proper self-esteem for both holiness and wholeness. Later I realized it was a vital part of my
training for a ministry of pastoral counseling.

And Then God Got Personal

My next experience with "If only" was much more personal
and painful. After ten years of village evangelism, I were ap-
pointed to a pastorate in Bangalore, a growing South Indian
metropolis noted for its universities, scientific research, and
commerce. It has now become the Silicon Valley of India's
burgeoning computer industry. During my six years there, I
experienced a personal inner healing which resulted in the
beginnings of the counseling ministry that would change the
whole direction of my life. I have given a detailed account of
this in *Healing of Memories*[4], but I want to emphasize one
aspect which is relevant here.

You may find this hard to believe, but up to that time I had
never sinned, never failed or fallen, never blown it with Helen
and the kids! Incredible, isn't it? Unbelievable? Yes, totally. Of
course, I had — many times, but *it wasn't really me.* I had the
most wonderful built-in emotional device deep down inside of
me. It was fully automatic. I didn't have to flip a switch to turn
it on. Every time I sinned or failed or fell, or blew it badly with
friends or family, this wonderful gadget turned itself on and a
little inner voice whispered, *"That's okay, David, don't worry
about it. You wouldn't have done that IF YOU HAD HAD A
DIFFERENT MOTHER."*

What a comfort that was — a soft Linus blanket I could
always fall back on in a time of failure. The most amazing thing

about it was that I had lived for so many years without ever really hearing my own "If only!" I had heard it repeatedly from the vast community of people I have just described, but had never heard it when I said it to myself! What a great shock to realize my own cop-out from assuming personal responsibility! Until I dealt with it, there could be no healing for my damaged emotions. Early in this process, I knew God's Spirit was saying to me, "That's gotta' go!"

With so many years of practicing my "If only," I didn't get rid of it overnight. But from then on, whenever my "If only" repeated itself, another voice spoke alongside it. Jesus' favorite word for the Holy Spirit in John's Gospel is *paraklete*, the "One who comes alongside us." Samuel Chadwick described this with a beautiful phrase, "the instant counteractivity of the Holy Spirit." So the Spirit would literally come alongside and remind me, "David, we don't do it that way anymore." I would then inwardly respond with a prayer for courage to assume full responsibility for my behavior, and to refuse to accept the "If only" excuse. Finally the time came when it was completely silenced.

In the Counseling Room

We left India in 1962 and began a thirty-year preaching-teaching-counseling ministry in the USA. At the church which was host to Asbury College and Seminary students, though the scene and the characters were different, the plot was the same: "If only I'd been born of different parents. If only my parents had not been so strict — or had been stricter. If only my parents had shown me more affection. If only I had not been an MK. If only I had the brains of my brother, or the beauty of my sister. If only I hadn't gotten sick the day of the exam. If only I had not been sexually abused. If only I had married someone else. If only I had not divorced, or had gotten a divorce much sooner. If only the bishop, or the superintendent, or the officials in the church had treated me fairly." The list was endless. At times I wondered what the B.A. and M.Div. degrees really stood for —

Bachelor of Arts or Builder of Alibis? Master of Divinity or Minister of Defense?

Please do not misunderstand what I am saying. There *is* such a thing as being a victim. In this imperfect, fallen, and sinful world, no one can deny that many people lay legitimate claim to being victims. Any day's evening news proves this beyond question. The Bible itself is filled with individuals, groups, and even nations who could accurately be called victims. And New Testament descriptions of Jesus being "moved with compassion" should forever cure us of purely mathematical formulas which consider all suffering the result of individual sins.

My own writings are filled with descriptions of the tragic emotional and spiritual consequences resulting from dysfunctional families, dys-graceful parenting in perfectionistic homes (including legalistic religious ones), and damaging physical, verbal, or sexual abuse . . . consequences which are often the result of the sins of others against us . . . consequences which are not only tragic but complex, and require counseling and special levels of inner healing which go deeper than being "born again" or "filled with the Spirit." I have been a pioneer in the field since I began stating these truths in the 1960s, long before they were readily accepted among evangelical Christians. So none of what I write here should in any way be construed to deny them.

Yet, even in the field of Christian counseling and recovery, we need to be reminded that although the Bible is filled with plenty of *victims*, it has no place for *victimology*. Rather, it stresses that there comes a time in the schedule of God's healing and recovery process when we all have to move beyond hurt to forgiveness, beyond wishful thinking to responsible action, beyond blame to belief. We move into the place where *victims can become victorious!*

Now a man named Lazarus was sick. He was from Bethany, the village of Mary and her sister Martha. . . . So the sisters sent word to Jesus, "Lord, the one You love is sick."

Jesus loved Martha and her sister and Lazarus. Yet when He heard that Lazarus was sick, He stayed where He was two more days. Then He said to His disciples, "Let us go back to Judea."

On His arrival, Jesus found that Lazarus had already been in the tomb for four days. . . . When Martha heard that Jesus was coming, she went out to meet Him, but Mary stayed at home.

"Lord," Martha said to Jesus, "if only You had been here, my brother would not have died. But I know that even now God will give You whatever You ask."

Jesus said to her, "Your brother will rise again."

Martha answered, "I know he will rise again in the resurrection at the last day."

Jesus said to her, "I am the resurrection and the life. He who believes in Me will live, even though he dies; and whoever lives and believes in Me will never die. Do you believe this?"

"Yes, Lord," she told Him, "I believe that You are the Christ, the Son of God, who was to come into the world." . . . And after she had said this, she went back and called her sister Mary. . . .

When Mary reached the place where Jesus was and saw Him, she fell at His feet and said, "Lord, if only You had been here, my brother would not have died."

When Jesus saw her weeping, and the Jews who had come along with her also weeping, He was deeply moved in spirit and troubled. . . .

Jesus wept. . . .

Then the Jews said, "See how He loved him." But some of them said, "Could not He who opened the eyes of the blind man have kept this man from dying?"

Jesus, once more deeply moved, came to the tomb. It was a cave with a stone laid across the entrance. "Take away the stone," He said.

"But, Lord," said Martha, "by this time there is a bad odor, for he has been there four days."

Then Jesus said, "Did I not tell you that if you believed, you would see the glory of God?" So they took away the stone. Then Jesus looked up and said, "Father, I thank You . . . that You always hear Me. . . ."

Jesus called in a loud voice, "Lazarus, come out!" The dead man came out, his hands and feet wrapped with strips of linen, and a cloth around his face.

Jesus said to them, "Take off the grave clothes and let him go."

Excerpts from John 11

"Lord, the one You love
is sick.... Yet when He heard
that Lazarus was sick,
He stayed where He was
two more days."

John 11:3, 6

2

The Mystery of Love versus Suffering

As you read the story of Lazarus' sickness, death, and resurrection in John 11, you cannot help but notice the "If onlys." The first one was spoken by Martha as she ran out on the road to meet Jesus before He even reached Bethany. That's to be expected of Martha. Overeager and overanxious, this was not the first time she had thrown an "If only" at Jesus. Once, when she felt Mary wasn't pulling her share of the load, she had scolded Him as if He were to blame for her negligence. "Lord, don't You care that my sister has left me to do the work by myself? Tell her to help me!" (Luke 10:40) In effect she was saying, "If only You cared enough about me, You'd have said something to Mary about it!" And so now, when she heard Jesus was finally approaching—late, of course, He was always stopping to heal some beggar on the road—she ran out to meet Him. "Lord," she whined, "if only You had been here, my brother would not have died." Yes, we expect that of Martha.

But wait a minute. Surprise! Until now contemplative, spiritual Mary had been in such deep grief she hadn't even left the house. But when she was told that Jesus had arrived, she went out and greeted Him with the very same words, "Lord, if only You had been here, my brother would not have died."

A few minutes later, Jesus countered their weak, hopeless "If only" with an entirely different kind of an "If." A strong, hopeful "if" by which He challenged them to change the direction of both their look and their outlook. And remember, He said it at the darkest and most devastating moment, right after Martha reminded him how long Lazarus had been dead and how bad his decomposed body would smell! "Did I not tell you that if you believed, you would see the glory of God?"

There they are side by side, "If only," and "If you will believe," the weakest and the strongest, the most hopeless and the most hopeful words, in sharp contrast. In the next several chapters we shall look at the details of this story and discover just how Jesus helped His dear friends move from their past-tense spirit of blaming Him to a present-tense spirit of believing in Him—the Great I AM of New Life.

The Mystery of Love and Suffering

We need to look at the background to this story, for it provides some reasons for the sisters' feelings of hurt, disappointment and, dare we say it, bitterness. John goes out of his way to stress Jesus' special relationship to the Bethany family of Mary, Martha, and their brother, Lazarus. It seems that their house was the only place Jesus could call home. Staying there was more than a matter of convenience, although Bethany was certainly well located as a quiet suburb less than two miles from Jerusalem. Like everyone else, Jesus needed a sense of belonging, and it was this family rather than His own which best filled that need. But deeper than this, He had a genuine love and affection for them. As John wrote, "Jesus loved Martha and her sister and Lazarus."

If those words had been written about any other religious leader in history, they could have damned him, for they might have been interpreted as morally incriminating. But when spoken about Jesus, the words are pure, beautiful, and heartwarming. Rather than arousing suspicion, they only deepen our admiration for His genuine humanness.

It is the fact of this special love which explains the unique wording of the message sent by the sisters when their brother fell ill, "Lord, the one You love is sick." Do you hear the real implications of it? I sense a bite to their words, a complaint as well as a request. It's a subtle, perhaps unconscious, expression of an age-old mystery, "Lord, we thought that You loved him; how has this happened to him?" It's the basic "Why?" we ask of God when things go wrong. We've all said it, at least thought it, when illness and tragedy struck us or our loved ones. I said it about my wife, Helen, some fifteen years ago. "Lord, she whom I love, and whom You love, has cancer."

How many times we've expressed something like it with aching hearts, "Lord, they whom we love are getting a divorce." What we mean by all such questions is that love and suffering seem contradictory and incompatible. "Lord, we thought You said that You loved us; how could this terrible thing be happening?" Or, "You have a strange way of showing Your love." Isn't this seeming contradiction the most basic hurdle in the whole healing process, and one we Christians must face up to sooner or later? It doesn't mean we are abnormal, doubting unbelievers; it only means we are normal, questioning human beings. Because we have been *wounded*, we are *wondering*.

Socrates said that all philosophy begins with the sense of wonder, and that this is what distinguishes us from other creatures. Animals suffer pain, but we humans are the only ones who *ponder* about it; we not only feel *pain*, but we feel *puzzled*. We *weep and wonder*, asking "Why?" in regard to the cause of our weeping. I believe that is what Mary and Martha's unique message is all about.

When It Became More Than Theory

Do you remember times when your bewildered heart sent a similar message to your Lord? How well I remember such a day back in 1948. Everything happened so quickly it left us shocked and numb. Our first son, healthy, ten-month-old David, had been cut down by fulminant bacillary dysentery in a matter of hours. We were told later that *fulminant* meant "to strike like lightning," and that certainly was accurate. We buried him in the reddish soil of Bidar the next morning. Sympathetic crowds of dear Indian friends and fellow missionaries streamed through our home for a couple of days. My parents and brother (also missionaries) were with us too. But after a few days we were all alone. Night came, and our three-year-old daughter, dazed and disturbed by the disappearance of her little brother, had finally gone to sleep. The empty silence was deafening. The single hurricane lantern cast eerie shadows on the walls and twenty-foot ceilings of the old mission bungalow. Helen was playing the piano and we began to sing one of our favorite hymns, "Spirit of God, Descend Upon My Heart." We did fine until the words of the fourth stanza seemed to jump out and gnaw at something deep within us.

Teach me to feel that Thou art always nigh;
Teach me the struggles of the soul to bear.
To check the rising doubt, the rebel sigh,
Teach me the patience of unanswered prayer.[1]

All at once my voice broke and I began to fight back the tears. Unwanted and unwelcome thoughts which I had pushed down suddenly erupted within me. Like molten lava, they spilled out into a bitter dialogue with God. "Lord, I don't understand. We left home and family and friends and came 10,000 miles to serve You as missionaries in India. We love You and we believe that You love us. Why did this happen? *How could You have let this happen to us?* Why? Why?"

In the coming days God had to teach both of us more about life and death, love and suffering. During our seminary days, we had studied all of this from the standpoint of philosophy and theology. We had some good logical answers and a whole list of memorized Scriptures as to why "bad things happen to good people." But we got ambushed by the wrenching emotional pain of it all. Pascal was right: "The heart has its reasons which reason knows nothing of."[2] A devout British missionary friend once said to me, "You know, at times like these, in some ways it would be easier if we were atheists, wouldn't it?" At first I was shocked, but then I realized he was right. For it's the very fact of knowing God personally, and knowing that He not only exists but also loves us, which makes the difficulty even greater. Certainly we believe that ultimately God will be a part of the solution; but in the beginning, He seems a part of the problem. For the contradiction is more than rational; it is relational. Now it's not so much a *philosophical question*, as it is a *family quarrel!*

Note how deeply personal every word of the sisters' message to Jesus is, "Lord, the one You love is sick." It reminds me of the prayer of the saintly Teresa of Avila. One day while protesting to God the seemingly unjust suffering of a good person, she claimed God said to her, "That's how I treat all My friends." To which she replied, "Well, Lord, now I understand why You have so few of them!"

No Special Immunity

The first thing Helen and I learned was that nowhere in Scripture are we given a strictly philosophical answer to the mystery of unjust suffering. We Christians need to forever fix in our minds that we live in a fallen, evil, and imperfect world. The fact that God loves us and we love Him *does not make us cosmic pets.* God's love for us does not give us a special immunity from tragedies, hurts, and pains. As the Apostle Paul wrote long ago, "It is plain to anyone with eyes to see that at the present time all created life groans in a sort of universal travail" (Romans 8:22, PH). Even nature has been affected by our fallenness and "groans" while awaiting a time of new creation. Jesus never said, "Come, follow Me, and I will give you a bed of roses." Or, "Come, be My disciple, and I will give you a special passport which will allow you to travel through this fallen world without ever being touched by its injustices, tragedies, and traumas." After all, none of Jesus' disciples died a natural death except the Apostle John, and he died as an exile on a lonely island. Jesus never promised us a *special immunity*, but He did promise a *special immanence—His presence.* He never promised an *answer*, but He promised *Himself, the Answerer.*

Our problems are not only about *something* — the event itself; they are about *Someone*, God Himself. Behind the questions from the puzzled *head*, "Why did it happen?" are the deeper questions of the pained *heart*, "Why did He allow it?" Or, "Why didn't He prevent it?"

After Lazarus died, this deeper aspect of the love and suffering mystery was brought up by some of the Jewish onlookers. When they saw Jesus weeping, they exclaimed, " 'See how He loved him!' But some of them said, 'Could not He who opened the eyes of the blind man have kept this man from dying?' " They seemed to be suggesting that love should have meant prevention, or at least intervention. Since Jesus had such great power and since He loved Lazarus so much, surely He should have expressed His love by preventing the tragedy from ever happening in the first place.

Even as I write this, faces arise in my memory, puzzled people from different backgrounds and varying levels of spiritual maturity who have shared their struggling faith with me on this very issue. . . .

  • Like the parents in India. They couldn't understand why, when an epidemic struck, their only child had died, while all of their neighbor's children had been spared.

  • Or the godly father in America who was dazed and confused by a terrible automobile accident which had killed his son. The man had faithfully served in his church, and even though it meant sacrificing income from his job, had gone on several short-term mission work teams. His son was a devout Christian and a brilliant ministerial student at our seminary. He was returning one night from doing volunteer work in a nearby city mission when a drunken driver ran a stop sign and hit him broadside. The driver escaped with only minor injuries.

  • And then there was the man in Estonia. When we prayed together, his body shook as uncontrollably as malaria patients I had seen in India. He told me he was remembering his years of torture in a Siberian concentration camp and couldn't understand how God would allow such suffering.

  • And I remember visiting the handsome, highly educated

young couple, members of our church in India, while she was recuperating in the hospital. There were no physical complications, but there was a serious crisis of faith as they struggled with the loss of a stillborn baby—for the second time!

• Or the many elderly saints, bedridden in nursing homes, who simply couldn't understand why they kept on living, in spite of their eagerness to be with Jesus and their daily prayers to God for "release."

• And the young divorcée in Britain, bitter because her unfaithful husband had not been converted, and the marriage had not been saved. She struggled with spiritual disillusionment because her well-meaning but unwise Christian friends had positively assured her he would become a believer—if she had enough faith.

• And how can I ever forget the young woman in her thirties who kept sobbing out her story of being sexually abused by an uncle. "I was only a little girl then and I cried out to God every time it happened, but God didn't stop him. You keep talking about a God of love, but I can't believe it. You're asking me to trust Him now, but how can I when He didn't hear me then?"

All of these converge on one thought: if God loves us, then He should *spare* us from calamaties, accidents, and tragedies. If God loves us, then He should *intervene* and *prevent* them from happening to us. And when He does not, it is a sign that there is something wrong with His love or with ours. Of course, sometimes we hear the opposite kind of testimony, "Ever since I became a Christian I've had no troubles at all." This reverse logic assumes that God's protection is a sure sign of His special love and favor.

There is a fundamental flaw in this whole line of thinking. I have spent hours and hours trying to help disillusioned Christians pick up the pieces of a shattered faith—faith which was broken by unrealistic expectations based on unbiblical presumptions. In recent years the problem has intensified because of the promises made by overzealous televangelists with their Health and Wealth Gospel. I know that God can, and sometimes does, intervene and save His children in certain situations. If He were not able to do so, He would be a prisoner of His own laws and a victim of His own ways. After all, those very laws are a part of His creation and He is sovereign. But God's regular and habitual way of running the universe is in accordance with these laws, and He has chosen to run it by order and not by whim. His laws are dependable because He is dependable, and that very dependability provides us the freedom to make moral choices. Scripture assures us that God *can* intervene, and when He does, it is properly called a "miracle." The problem comes when we say we can judge either the degree of God's love for us or the extent of our faith in Him by whether or not He intervenes when we face tragedy.

Not Even Jesus Was Spared

The mystery of love and suffering is not found in guaranteed immunity, protection, or intervention, but in a totally different direction. At the very height of Jesus' suffering on the cross, as He was forsaken by people and seemingly by God Himself, the religious leaders mocked Him saying, "He trusts in God. Let God rescue Him now if He wants Him, for He said, 'I am the Son of God' " (Matthew 27:43). Here is another great "If." If God would intervene and rescue Him, it would prove that He loved Him, and that Jesus was pleasing to God; but if He didn't, it would prove the opposite. Here is the same kind of false thinking applied to our Lord Himself. We know that God did not deliver Jesus. Rather, He did something much better, and we too shall find His solution to the problem in our lives along a better way.

When the people asked Jesus the "Why?" of the man who had been born blind, He told them, "so that the work of God might be displayed in his life" (John 9:3). That was essentially the same answer He gave regarding Lazarus' sickness and death, "It is for God's glory" (John 11:4). Let's be sure we do not misunderstand this as an oversimplistic answer intended to shut down our pain or grief. Christianity is not a refined form of stoicism which asks us to deny our emotions and repress any negative expression of feeling. We are not called to be one of God's frozen-chosen with a fixed smile, and an automatic "Praise the Lord" for every situation. Jesus' behavior when Lazarus died completely destroys that caricature. He was so deeply moved with sorrow that He openly wept at the grave of His friend. We recognize the cross to be His ultimate identification with all the world's victims, and His Resurrection to be the ultimate power enabling them to become victors. So let no one mistake the Christian answer to the mystery of suffering as simplistic. In reality, it is very profound and costly.

An Even Greater Mystery

When Jesus heard that Lazarus was ill, He did something that added greater mystery. After John tells us, "Jesus loved Martha and her sister and Lazarus," he adds, "Yet when He heard that Lazarus was sick, He stayed where He was two more days" (11:6). How very strange. Instead of responding to their 911 call, canceling everything, and immediately starting out for Bethany, Jesus took His time and stayed two extra days!

Have you ever had times when God not only didn't seem to care, but also didn't seem to know what He was doing? On the surface, Jesus' deliberate two-day delay just doesn't make sense. But take a closer look, and you'll discover Jesus knew exactly what He was doing. Figure it out: it was a day's journey from Bethany to the place where Jesus was ministering. So it took the messenger one day to get there. Then Jesus stayed on two days longer. The trip back took Jesus and the disciples another day, a total of four days. "On His arrival Jesus found that Lazarus had already been in the tomb for four days." From the very beginning Jesus knew something that neither the messenger nor the disciples knew — that Lazarus was not just sick but was already dead by the time the message got to him. Jesus knew exactly what He was doing and why He was doing it, so that God could bring even greater glory out of it all. In the words of Bishop Handley Moule, "There is no situation so chaotic that God cannot, from that situation, create something that is surpassingly good. He did it at Creation. He did it at the cross. He is doing it today."[3]

It was our privilege to be a part of the 1994 Gaither Praise Gathering in Indianapolis. Our hearts were thrilled by the outstanding Christian speakers and musicians who took part. But the two persons who moved us the most suffered from physical disabilities and speech defects. One was a teenager, Gianna Jessen, who was born in an abortion clinic, the survivor of an unsuccessful saline abortion. The attending nurse noticed the aborted baby was still alive and rushed her to a hospital. Although she weighed only two pounds, she miraculously survived and spent the first several months of her life there. Eventually she was placed in foster care and was soon diagnosed with cerebral palsy. She was given no chance of walking, crawling, or even sitting up. Today, as a joyful teenager, she convinces people all over the country through her singing and personal testimony that every single day is a reason to celebrate life. "You see, God had different plans for me. By His grace, faithful prayers, and consistent love, and the dedication of my foster mother, I proved the doctors wrong!" She enjoys hiking, playing softball, is involved in Christian Youth Theater in San Diego, and is active in a pro-life ministry.

David Ring was born with cerebral palsy. In spite of his serious handicaps, he is now a husband and father, and has become a well-known preacher who travels everywhere holding evangelistic services. After giving his testimony, he started singing the verses to the old Gospel song, "Victory in Jesus." At his request, the crowd of 12,000 people joined him in singing the chorus! Many felt it was the most moving experience of the conference.

Both Gianna and David are being used to win many people to Christ. They are victims in the truest sense of the word: one the victim of another's sinful choice, the other a victim of an accident during birth. No one has more right to say "If only," and spend the rest of their lives in bitter blaming, than these two. Instead, they have grasped Christ's challenging, "If you will believe." So we, as well as they, now experience "the glory of God" reflected in their radiance and joy. As I sat and listened to these victorious victims, the Lord's words to Paul came to my mind, "My grace is sufficient for thee: for My strength is made perfect in weakness." And Paul's exultant response, "Most gladly therefore will I rather glory in my infirmities that the power of Christ may rest upon me" (2 Corinthians 12:9, KJV).

I also felt that Gianna and David were living examples of something E. Stanley Jones used to say about the Christian answer to the problem of evil and suffering. "God does not want us to just *find the answer*. He wants us to *become the answer!*"

That's what Jesus wanted for Martha and Mary. He wanted them to *become* the answer by actively participating *in* the answer. And He knew that if they believed, that is exactly what would happen. This meant, of course, that He had to take them on a spiritual journey that would move them *from blaming to believing*.

Jesus wants to do that for all of us "If only-ers." My prayer is that the Living Word, the Risen Christ Himself, will take each of us by the hand, and lead us step by step on this same pilgrimage. If we will allow Him to do this, to borrow an incisive phrase from Leslie Weatherhead,

> Although we will not be at the end of our journey,
> we will be at the end of our wandering.[4]

"If You had been here,
my brother would not have died."

John 11:21, 32

3

Moving into the Present

*P*arade magazine ran a review of the book, *Brando: Songs My Mother Taught Me*, in which the Oscar-winning actor Marlon Brando told how his "tragic family shaped his life." He described his father as a promiscuous traveling salesman, "an alcoholic who tortured me emotionally and made my mother's life miserable." His mother also "was an alcoholic whom I loved but who ignored me." Regarding his love life he wrote, "I have always been lucky with women. There have been many in my life, though I hardly ever spent more than a couple of minutes with any of them. I've had far too many affairs to think of myself as a normal, rational man." Brando was always close to his sisters "because we were all scorched by the experience of growing up in the furnace that was my family."

The article is a classic example of what has been termed a "pathography" — the chronicle of a celebrated figure's flaws and failure from a psychoanalytical view. It is also a perfect illustration of the past-tense viewpoint. The article concludes with a picture of the seventy-year-old star and his words, *"If I had been loved and cared for differently, I would have been a different person."*[1]

One of the most serious problems with "If only" is that it results in living in the past tense — a tense which represents behavior and events which have already taken place and cannot be changed. As we sometimes say, "Well, things might have been different 'if only' this or that had (or hadn't) happened. Anyhow that's history." And to stress our point we often sigh and quote Whittier's lines,

> For of all sad words of tongue or pen,
> The saddest are these: "It might have been."

Used in this way, "If only" fixes our gaze on those aspects of the past which are unalterable. That's why it is not only weak but also worthless. It never does anything except to take a bad situation and make it worse. It never helps anyone break the chains of an evil habit. It never urges anyone to reopen a door which seems to be closed. It never brings back a day that has been lost. It never restores a shattered dream, but only reinforces its brokenness. It closes the book on any change and nails the lid on the casket of hope.

"If only" wastes our energy by concentrating on past events we have no power to change. It robs us of the ability to face realities of the present and possibilities of the future. It fails to take into account that while certain facts of the past cannot be changed, our perception of them can be. They can be reframed, seen through new lenses, and understood from a different viewpoint. "If only" is a *past-tense viewpoint* which permanently freezes life. The way Brando used the perfect tense illustrates this hopelessness so clearly. "If I would have been _____ then, I would be _____ now." His meaning is obvious, "It's not my fault, and it's too late to change."

If Only, Past and Future

In a similar way Martha and Mary told Jesus, "Lord, *if only* You had been here *then*, everything would be fine *now*. But now it's too late." Jesus had to somehow get them to change the *tense* of their outlook. He knew only this would change the *spirit* of their outlook. The big fallacy in their "If only" was that it left out the present power of the Living Christ.

So Jesus tried to get them to switch from their powerless

past-tense "If only" to His powerful present-tense "If you be-lieve." Martha caught on to what Jesus was trying to do and began to struggle with it. Hurrah for Martha. I get tired of all the Martha put-downs, including my own in the last chapter. Do you realize that Martha broke all the traditions of her religion and culture by not waiting in the house like Mary did? She rushed out to meet Jesus on the road. And in the same way, she did her best not only to express her despair but also to venture out in faith. "But I know that even now God will give You whatever You ask" (11:22). *"Even now"* — a hint of her inner battle to escape from the prison of the past into the freedom of the present.

But she can't quite make it, so look what happens. When Jesus assures her, "Your brother will rise again," Martha does what a lot of us "If only-ers" do. She switches from a dismal past-tense "If only" to a distant future-tense "If only" and says, "I know he will rise again in the Resurrection at the last day." As if to say, "Of course, Lord, *if only* it was the coming great Day of Resurrection, then I know he would rise and live again."

Missing the Present Tense

I once worked with a fellow minister who missed the present. He talked a great deal about the wonderful days of the past: "If only" things were like the "good old days." But those of us who remembered being with him during those past times had heard his continual grumbling and murmuring then about how bad things really were. It was only much later, after it all became the past, that he "If onlyed" about its grandeur. Or, he would turn things around in the opposite direction and wistful-ly "If only" about a kind of "golden age" to come in the distant future. But then, when that future arrived and became the present, it was the same old story. Once again he would "If only" about the great days of the past! He had a rather simple problem: he lived in the past and the future. The former was filled with inaccurate memories, the latter with unrealistic thinking. *He never really lived in the present, experiencing both its realities and its possibilities for joy or sorrow.*

The Screwtape Letters by C.S. Lewis is a series of imaginary letters by Uncle Screwtape, an experienced senior devil in hell. He is advising his nephew, Wormwood, a young demon who is just beginning his work on earth by tempting a man who has recently become a Christian. He has several suggestions that apply to our subject:

> The humans live in time, but our Enemy [God] destines them to eternity. He therefore, I believe, wants them to attend chief-ly to two things, to eternity itself and to that point of time they call the Present. For the Present is the point at which time touches eternity. . . .
>
> Our business is to get them away from the eternal and from the Present. With this in view, we sometimes tempt a human . . . to live in the Past. But this is of limited value. . . . It is far better to make them live in the Future . . . it is unknown to them, so that in making them think about it, we make them think of unrealities. In a word, the Future is, of all things, the *least like* eternity.[2]

Screwtape also has diabolical advice on something which usually goes along with living in the future: failing to act in the present by postponing it until the future, or by deluding ourselves into thinking that because we've given something our attention, we've accomplished it, when all we've actually done is to think or talk about it.

> The great thing is to prevent his doing anything. As long as he does not convert it into action, it does not matter how much he thinks about [it]. Let the little brute wallow in it. Let him, if he has any bent that way, write a book about it. . . . Let him do anything but act. No amount of piety in his imagination and affections will harm us if we can keep it out of his will. . . . The more often he feels without acting, the less he will be able ever to act, and, in the long run, the less he will be able to feel.[3]

All during my ministry I have met counselees who seem to have succumbed to Screwtape's deadly temptation. Life would be completely different and they wouldn't have these problems. "If only" something hadn't happened back in the *past.* Or, things are going to be different someday in the *future.* Their favorite phrases are either "If only" or "Someday." Someday "I plan to," "I intend to," "I know I need to forgive and I will," or "I'm going to stop — or start — doing that." How many times I have heard an alcoholic use future "If only" phrases similar to those. Perhaps you recall that a few years ago a recovered alcoholic wrote a best-selling book entitled, *I'll Quit Tomorrow!* Sometimes, if I felt the situation was serious enough, when I heard the phrase, "I've been thinking about doing this or that," I tried to shock the person into action by asking, "How long do you intend to go on just thinking about it?"

I occasionally remind my counselees of the deadly effect of living in an "If only" future. Jim Fixx did more than anyone else to popularize jogging as the simplest way to maintain fitness and good health. And he practiced what he preached, running and jogging an average of ten miles a day. No wonder the world was shocked with disbelief when he suddenly died of a massive heart attack! His ex-wife told reporters that though he had talked about it and someday intended to, he never saw a doctor or had a checkup.

"I AM" Today

After Martha, shifted her "If only" from the past to the future, she appeared to be inwardly struggling with the possible implications of what Jesus had said. It was then that He uttered one of the most precious and oft-quoted truths in Scripture. How remarkable that He said it to her rather than Mary. Yes, it was Martha, the eager beaver, sometimes blunt and brash, but always honest and open, whom Jesus rewarded by giving these wonderful words, "I AM the resurrection and the life. He who believes in Me will live."

This is the answer to Martha and to the the tragic tendency of all "If only-ers" who tend to miss living in the present. For Jesus is the great "I AM." In the Gospel of John He uses that phrase six other times to describe Himself. Each one stresses a different aspect of who He is, but He is always the I AM, our Eternal Contemporary.

I AM the Bread of Life (6:35).
I AM the Light of the world (8:12).
I AM the Good Shepherd (10:11).
I AM the Gate (10:9).
I AM the Way, the Truth and the Life (14:6).
I AM the True Vine (15:1).

One day He even told the startled crowd, "Before Abraham was born, I AM!" (John 8:58) Throughout the Bible God always confronts us as the Present One in the present tense. When Moses had his great experience with God, it was the fact that the burning bush was *not consumed* that riveted his attention; it kept on burning, present tense. And when God ordered him to go and deliver the Israelites out of Pharaoh's slavery, he asked God whom he should say had sent him. "God said to Moses, 'I AM who I AM. This is what you are to say to the Israelites: I AM has sent me to you' " (Exodus 3:14). That is why *now* is the Bible's favorite *time* word, "Now is the time of God's favor, now is the day of salvation" (2 Corinthians 6:2). Jesus is the I AM, alive, well and active, who wants to redeem, heal, and restore to new life, starting *now*.

In order to move Martha and Mary from their "If only," He had to free them from their bondage to both the "too late" of the past and the "maybe someday" of the future. He wanted them to fix their eyes on Him, the Eternal, Present-Tense Contemporary. So immediately after His "I AM," He asked Martha, "Do you believe this?" She struggled with the *possibility* of Lazarus' resurrection now. But she was a woman of such remarkable honesty that she would not declare a faith she didn't have. However, she affirmed what she did have — full trust in the Person of Christ. "Yes, Lord, I believe that You are the Christ, the Son of God, who was to come into the world." She was no longer *glancing* at past and future "If onlys." She was now *gazing* at the powerful Presence of Christ, and this was generating a whole new level of faith. Soon Mary would join her and they would be ready to see "the glory of God."

Just how did Jesus move them into a present-tense view-point of believing? Perhaps it would help if we saw how He did it in a similar situation, described in Luke 24:13-35. Two of His followers were walking from Jerusalem to their village of Emmaus, two days after Jesus had been crucified. In their deep grief, they were discussing the tragic details of His trial, death, and burial. Jesus joined them but they didn't recognize Him. They were amazed at His ignorance of what had happened, and when He inquired about it, they once again went over the story with Him. The depth of their sadness and disillusionment is heard in their words, "But we *had hoped* that He was the One." Again the past-perfect tense—you can't have a more hopeless "If only" than that.

Jesus used words and actions to bring them out of the past and into the present. First, He taught them through His words, reinterpreting everything they had told Him in a completely different way, by relating it to the Old Testament Scriptures. In His words He reframed the past events and gave them new meaning. Then He did something. In His simple act of break-ing bread at the supper table, they saw and recognized Him for who He really was! After that, in spite of the fact they had just walked seven miles to Emmaus, and darkness had set in, "they got up and returned at once to Jerusalem!" They simply had to tell the disciples what they had *heard* and *seen*. Their frozen "If only" of the past had thawed out as His presence made their "hearts burn within" them and flowed right into a joyous, exciting present!

Jesus followed that same pattern in moving Martha and Mary from the past into the present. Oswald Chambers says, "The root of faith is the knowledge of a Person."[4] We come to know people by their words and deeds. Jesus had already spo-ken His wonderful words, reminding them that He was the Great I AM. Now His words must "become flesh" by an act, something He would do.

Surely we would have expected Him to begin by doing

something incredible to reveal His divinity — maybe appearing as a blaze of Living Light as He did on the Mount of Transfiguration. They would then see "the glory" and be overwhelmed into faith. Instead, He did the very opposite. He began by revealing His full humanity at the very point where all of us are at our weakest.

Jesus Wept

The Gospel of John was written primarily for Greeks who believed that the chief characteristic of God was *apatheia*, the total inability to feel any emotion. To them, God was "the Unmoved Mover" of the universe, isolated, passionless and, therefore, compassionless. Theologians have argued about this for centuries. God is immutable, they insist; therefore, God cannot really *feel* our pain. He is perfect; therefore, He is untouched and unmoved.

In their remarkable book, *In His Image,* Dr. Paul Brand and Philip Yancey present this issue in a different and helpful light. They say that such an idea is too Western, too allied to Greek philosophy. The Hebrew viewpoint is quite different. They suggest there may be a way to put both of these truths together by considering the human brain with its remarkable paradox concerning pain. Because the brain has no nerve endings which record pain, the brain itself cannot feel any pain. Once a brain surgeon gets through the skull he can cut anything he wants within the brain, and there will be no pain. Yet, the pain center of the entire body is in the brain. All pain — from our little fingers to our big toes, from every internal organ to every external section of skin — all pain from any place in the body passes through the brain, and that's how we *feel* it. Anesthesia doesn't actually stop the nerve ending from *feeling* the pain; it stops the brain from *recording* it, and so we don't *feel* it. Perhaps, they say, God and our pain are something like that. Because Christ is the "Head of the Body," we can in one sense say *He feels no pain.* But in another sense we can say *He feels all pain,* since all pain passes through Him. Thus we can truly say

He feels the whole world's pain and hurt, including yours and mine. In this way, Brand and Yancey suggest, seemingly contradictory truths can be held together.[5]

To John's Greek readers, for God to show emotion would deny His omnipotence and be unworthy of what a deity was supposed to be. But that didn't phase John, for here, in living color and stereophonic sound, he reveals a totally different picture of God. John 11:35, "Jesus wept," is the shortest verse in the Bible. When I was a boy in Sunday School, it was one of my favorites. I could always use it to get credit for another Bible verse and earn an additional star on my memory chart! That is, until the teacher wouldn't let me quote it anymore. In those days I never dreamed how BIG that little verse really is, how important and how tremendous the theological truth wrapped up in two small words. It has taken me a lifetime to realize what a massive door swings upon those two tiny hinges. It is the door which opens into the very heart of God, revealing that behind this universe is a *caring heart of suffering love.*

"When Jesus saw her weeping, and the Jews who had come along with her also weeping, He was *deeply moved in spirit and troubled.* . . . Jesus, once more *deeply moved,* came to the tomb" (11:33, 38, italics added). The *King James Version* says He "groaned in Himself," and Phillips renders it, "He was deeply moved and visibly distressed." Yes, Jesus wept so openly, so loudly, so vulnerably, so unself-consciously, so sympathetically, so empathetically that the people around Him said, "See how He loved him" (11:36).

In his commentary on John, William Barclay discusses the difficulty of understanding the true meaning of the word *embrimasthai,* "deeply moved" or "groaned." He informs us that in classical Greek, one of the common uses for the word was "the snorting of a horse." He quotes Rieu's translation as nearest the original, "He gave way to such distress of spirit as made the body tremble," and says it can only mean that "such deep emotion seized Jesus that an involuntary groan was wrung from His heart."[6]

To get an even fuller understanding, we should combine this

word with the one used twelve times in the other Gospels when it speaks of Jesus as having or being moved with compassion. The Greek root word for compassion, *splanchna*, means the "intestines or bowels," thought to be the inward parts from which the strongest human emotions arose. We still use the idea in our phrase "gut-level feeling" or "gut reaction." So when the Bible says Jesus was "moved with compassion" or that He "groaned in His Spirit," we are being told that His gut was wrenched and His heart torn open. Henri Nouwen tells us that the word

> is related to the Hebrew word for compassion, *rachamin*, which refers to the womb of Yahweh. Compassion is such a deep, central and powerful emotion in Jesus that it can only be described as a movement of the womb of God. There all the divine tenderness and gentleness lies hidden. There, God is father and mother, brother and sister, son and daughter. There all feelings, emotions and passions are one in divine love.[7]

How often we have all asked, "Where *was* God when that dreadful thing happened? Where *is* God when we soak the pillow with our sobs? When the loss, the loneliness, and the painful memories cut through us like a surgeon's knife without anesthesia?" Jesus assures us where God is — *He is alongside us, moved with compassion, weeping with us and for us with a broken heart.* Here is the ultimate answer to the mystery of evil and suffering. *Emmanuel — God with us. God for us. God in it all the way with us as one of us.*

Let us personalize it so as to understand its full meaning. Here is God in Christ, the Great I AM, totally identifying, understanding, and hurting with me right where I am in my pain, suffering, and victimization. The Incarnate God, my Elder Brother, Companion, Unrelenting Lover, and Fellow Sufferer, who at great cost to Himself desires to become my Savior, Healer, and Restorer of new life. The Great I AM is weeping as I am weeping. That sight was enough to tear Martha and Mary away from both past and future ruminations, and bring them right into the present. And that tremendous thought can bring us right along with them.

But, in one sense, isn't all we have been saying actually in the past tense? The story is almost 2,000 years old and the Jesus of whom we have been speaking is the Jesus of history. How is all this to become truly and literally present tense for us now? This weeping, suffering Jesus then "ascended into heaven," where "He always lives to intercede" for us (Hebrews 7:25). Or, as Paul puts it, "Christ Jesus, who died — more than that, who was raised to life — is at the right hand of God and is also interceding for us" (Romans 8:34). And all this is made contemporary when the Jesus of history becomes the Christ of our personal experience through the Holy Spirit He has given to us. The early church fathers stated it so beautifully when they asserted that the *ascended Son* continues in heavenly intercession *for us*, while the *descended Spirit* continues in earthly counsel *with us*.

We see this in Romans 8 where words for this present work of Christ and the Holy Spirit are used interchangeably. The Holy Spirit is the *paraklete*, the One called alongside. And Romans 8:25-27 assures us that He helps us with our cripplings, infirmities, weaknesses, and pains. Just as Jesus "groaned" in sympathy with Martha and Mary, and just as we groan amidst our sufferings, "in the same way the Spirit Himself intercedes for us with groans that words cannot express." Nothing is more therapeutic and more comforting than this. The word *comfort* is not a weak word connoting mere sympathy or understanding. It comes from the Latin *con fortis*, "with fortitude," and means "to give strength."

I saw an inspiring example of this on a television program many years ago. A young mother in her mid-thirties, Laurel Lee, was being interviewed about her experiences recorded in her books, *Walking Through the Fire*, and *Signs of Spring*. As a mother of three, she had fallen victim to cancer. The situation became so difficult that her husband could no longer face it. One day, when she returned from a treatment at the hospital, she found he had put the house up for sale and started divorce proceedings. Things went from bad to worse. Finally, she rented a small house and together with her kids moved in. In remarkably creative ways, she and the children made a game out of the difficulties. Her oldest son, age six, had to sleep in the closet. She bought railroad decals, put them all over the closet, and pretended that the shelf was the upper berth of a pullman carriage on a train. Then she gave him a flashlight and put him in a sleeping bag. He thought it was a lot of fun.

Her cancer would go into remission and then return, so the future was quite uncertain. David Hartman, who was interviewing her, was amazed. "How do you do it?" he asked. "What are your resources?"

She replied immediately, "It's my Christian faith. I've been a Christian for nine years and I've learned to live in the present. That has kept me from being overcome, and has made me an overcomer. Actually, I'm thankful for it all. I just live for every day and enjoy the present moment. I used to always live in the future. 'Wait till the weekend, Wait till vacation,' I'd say. Now every moment is precious. Knowing God's presence helps me push the *up* button on the elevator and live looking up, instead of the *down* button!"

"Jesus wept."
John 11:35

4

The Ultimate Victim

Before bedtime each evening, a young mother read from a children's Bible storybook to her little boy. The book was written in simple language and was illustrated by colorful drawings. The child was fascinated by the stories of Christmas, Jesus' birth, the shepherds, the star, and the wisemen. He was excited when the little boy gave his lunch to Jesus so He could feed 5,000 people, and he assured his mother he would have done that if he'd been there. He laughed with delight when Jesus told the stormy Sea of Galilee, "Hush, be quiet!"

But he got very still when he was told of the betrayal and trial of Jesus, and how they nailed Him to a cross along with two robbers. His face darkened, tears filled his eyes, and he finally burst out angrily, "O Mama, if only God had been there, He wouldn'ta let them do it to Him!"

But that's the glory of the story, isn't it? He was there! In some inexpressible, mysterious way, there at the cross, "God was reconciling the world to Himself in Christ" (2 Corinthians 5:19). It was God's love, God's pain, God's suffering, and God's sacrifice on that cross which made it all possible. Charles Wesley's great hymn "And Can It Be" beautifully and daringly states this almost incomprehensible truth.

> And can it be that I should gain
> An interest in the Savior's blood?

Died He for me, who caused His pain?
For me, who Him to death pursued?
Amazing Love! How can it be
That thou, My God, shouldst die for me?

'Tis mystery all! Th' Immortal dies!
Who can explore His strange design?[1]

The cross is at the heart of our faith, for there God's love was shown in Christ's ultimate identification with sinners, where "God made Him who had no sin to be sin for us, so that in Him we might become the righteousness of God" (2 Corinthians 5:21).

But we impoverish the Gospel when we confine the effects of the cross to the forgiveness and cleansing of our sins, as infinitely great as that is. At this point I want to express my great debt to Dr. Frank Lake for emphasizing the importance of the cross for a truly biblical theology of counseling. In his incomparable book, *Clinical Theology*[2], Dr. Lake underlines the significance of the cross for the Christian counselor. He maintains that pastoral care is defective unless it deals thoroughly with the *evils* we have suffered as well as the *sins* we have committed. While I do not agree with some of his psychoanalytic applications, I want to give him credit for his profound biblical insights. In this chapter, I will be referring to many of his ideas.

Lake stresses that in the cross we see Christ's ultimate identification not only with all guilty sinners, but also with all the innocent sufferers of the world. He not only bore the penalty and consequences due all who have *sinned*, but He also experienced the whole range of physical, mental, emotional, and spiritual pain borne by those who have been *sinned against*. He totally identified with all *innocent victims* as well as all *guilty sinners*.

For those who know their problem is primarily due to their own sinning, there is nothing but "wonder, love, and praise" for the peace of His forgiveness achieved upon the cross. But I have seen increasing numbers of broken people who were cruelly sinned against and their spiritual capacities deeply wounded during the early years of life. They have an added dimension to their faith problem. When Jesus recognized that in this world occasions for sin inevitably happen, He then uttered His "woe" of warning to those who "cause these little ones to sin" (Matthew 18:6-7; Luke 17:1-2). The damaged emotions of those sinned against have so distorted their concepts/feelings they find it almost impossible to believe from their hearts that God is good. They also find it nearly impossible to trust a God whose world allows such innocent suffering. Like Job of old, they have a quarrel with God, since their suffering was not the result of their own sin. As sinners, their need is to be reconciled to God through forgiveness. But as sufferers, they need to be reconciled to God by clear evidence that He cares and shares and understands their suffering. Christ's cross and resurrection is God's gracious answer to both needs. *In the cross, Christ became the Ultimate Atonement for sin and the Ultimate Victim of suffering. In the Resurrection He is the Ultimate Triumph over both.*

To John all the miracles were considered "signs" pointing to some great truth. The raising of Lazarus is a living parable of what was soon to follow—Christ's death and resurrection. Jesus' sorrow as He wept with the mourners is a preview, a prefigurement of His ultimate identification with all the sorrow of the world. And Lazarus' resurrection foretells Christ's own triumph over death and the tomb, the final Christian answer to the "mystery of iniquity" and suffering.

In the cross and resurrection, all the powers of evil, which operate in the shadows behind chosen sin and innocent suffering, are defeated and dethroned. For in the Crucifixion, Christ deliberately and voluntarily allowed Himself to become not only an *atonement* for sin but also an *innocent victim* of the sinful choices of others. In His resurrection, He triumphed over both, so that now we too can become *victors over both*. If we leave this aspect out of our preaching, teaching, and counseling, we are failing to tell hurting people what they desperately need to hear.

The Healer of Our Hurts
Is the Feeler of Our Hurts

In chapter 2 I mentioned an incest victim's bitter cry against God for failing to hear her childhood prayers for help. Both this woman and her sister had been sexually molested by an uncle. They attended one of our weekend seminars, "Emotional and Spiritual Wholeness." During an afternoon session on "Forgiveness: The Heart of Healing," they both expressed their deep resentments against God—and me—for even daring to suggest they needed to forgive the one they blamed for ruining their lives. Phillips' paraphrase of Hebrews 12:15, "a bitter spirit which can poison the lives of many others," had literally come true in their relationships, especially with men. Both of them were quite open about their bitterness and felt that their tragic and traumatic "If only" gave them every "right" to be resentful.

However, at the close of the next morning's session, one of the sisters accepted my invitation and came to the altar for a special time of healing prayer. Her hateful spirit melted away as God "poured out His love" into her heart "by the Holy Spirit" (Romans 5:5). These words were written by Paul in the context of the cross. But what possible word from the cross could God speak to a victim of sexual abuse? The word came when she heard that in the earliest paintings of the Crucifixion, Jesus was always naked. Thus Christ, in His humiliation and disgrace, had identified with all victims of the shame of nakedness. It began to dawn on her that Jesus understood the pain of shameful exposure, because He had been through it Himself. Therefore, He understood why she was so hurt and angry, and having such difficulty forgiving. Jesus was not judging or condemning her anger against God, but was weeping with her and for her. Becoming aware of this cracked her defenses, and God's forgiving grace was able to enter into the hidden caverns of her damaged spirit. Regretfully, her sister did not respond, but became all the more angry. And she felt betrayed by her sister for leaving her to nurse the hurt and hate all by herself.

I had never realized this aspect of Christ's passion until Helen and I were privileged to have Corrie ten Boom with us in our home for three days, when she preached at our church in Bangalore, India. One morning at breakfast I asked her what was the worst thing she had suffered in the German concentration camps during the Holocaust. She paused for a few moments and then gave an answer completely different from what we were expecting. "It was the nakedness, so often having to be naked before all those jeering soldiers. That was the worst of all!" Yes, even that was part of our Lord's total identification with the world's suffering.

The One Who Wipes Our Tears Also Weeps with Us

The question "Why?" is constantly asked by all who suffer in innocence, their lives crippled or crushed by the sins of others. Waves of injustice drive them back into seas of doubt about a God of love. When we study Christ's Passion, we too are pushed to ask "Why?" at every detail. In His passion and death, Christ suffered every possible injustice. Although He was totally innocent, for no one could find any fault in His behavior, He was the victim of every *inequity* as well as every *iniquity*. Pilate, Herod, and Caiaphas the high priest were guilty of denying to Jesus the common justice of their own laws. And God, who wanted the Son to be identified with all who suffer as victims of injustice, permitted it to happen that way. He "did not spare His own Son, but gave Him up for us all" (Romans 8:32). God did not exempt Jesus from being caught in the inescapable, evil complexities of this fallen and imperfect world. In the first Christian sermon ever preached, Peter said it plainly, "This man [Jesus] was handed over to you by God's set purpose and foreknowledge; and you, with the help of wicked men, put Him to death by nailing Him to the cross" (Acts 2:23).

If Jesus was to be fully identified with us, then He too had to be a victim, because *we are all victims in one way or another*. We all suffer from the consequences of choices *we* did not make, accidents *we* did not cause, genetic defects *we* did not create, emotional dysfunctions *we* could not escape, spiritual deformities *we* did not initiate, and judgments *we* did not deserve. And most of us, at some deep, cavernous level of our being, have cried out in agony at a supposedly all-powerful, all-loving God who allowed it to happen.

Humiliation

Consider some of the ways Jesus identified fully with our sufferings. Think of all those who are slapped, mocked, made fun of, put down, and who suffer the pain of attack, physically or verbally, on their own self-worth. As Jesus moved from the courtroom to the tomb, the soldiers, the crowd, the priests, bystanders, passersby, even the two thieves being crucified on each side of him, "hurled insults at Him" (Luke 23:39).

I often counsel people who are filled with deep hurt, rage, and the desire to inflict pain. They may tell me their story in clinical detail, without a flicker of emotion. But when I gently probe more deeply, asking, "What's the worst thing that comes to your mind? What slow-motion-video-replay-memory recurs most often and brings the most emotional pain?" a change takes place. Their eyes become moist and their tone of voice changes to a different key. As they relate painful scenes in quivering words, one theme stands out above all the others, *humiliation*. More painful than severe physical bruises on the body were the slaps in the face or blows to the head. Somehow the face and head are deeply connected to our personal identity and self-esteem, and abuse to them is very demeaning and dehumanizing.

Humiliation is also directly related to assault on sexual organs. Such abuse literally violates privacy, renders victims naked, and robs them of their most secret, precious possession. Adults have shaken with painful rage as they remembered, no, relived, the nauseous shame. I believe there is also an intricate connection between sexual identity and the personal identity of the face. How often I have heard a tearful incest victim say, "When he violated me there was nothing I could do but *cover my face* with a pillow and cry." The resulting distortions of their sexual attitudes and behavior, their deep sense of shame, false guilt, and low self-esteem all needed to be healed.

And then there are the *humiliating* and *belittling* messages which even now reverberate in the mental circuits of their victims. They bring a renewed sense of failure, low self-worth, and incompetence which literally keeps saying, *"Be little!"*

- "Son, if there's a wrong way to do it, you'll find it."
- "I was pregnant with you when we married. On our honeymoon night, your dad sat on the edge of the edge of the bed and cried."
- "If it weren't for you children, I could have been a singing star; but, of course, my children are my songs."
- "There you go—you've messed your pants right here in the mall. Well, you can just stay dirty and smelly. You deserve to suffer for a while."
- "You're going to turn out to be a worthless bum, just like your Uncle Mack."
- "No wonder you don't have any friends. As soon as they get to know you, they don't like you."

These terribly destructive statements are not attempts to correct *wrongdoing*, a necessary part of parental discipline. Rather, they are all inferences of *bad being*. It is not what you have done but who you are. Jesus endured verbal abuse, sarcastic statements, and mocking insults, not for what He had *done* but for who He *was*—"Son of God," "King of the Jews," "Messiah." These names were used to belittle Him.

Defenselessness

Christ also identifies with those who are defenseless, without physical strength, or who have lost all their natural rights. Jesus, the sturdy young carpenter whose arms were made

strong from carrying wood, was so drained of s.   .gth that He
fell under the weight of the cross, too exhausted even to carry
it with dignity. Just a few days before, like a King He
requisitioned a donkey to ride into the capital city; as the
Master Teacher He requisitioned a room for a meal with His
disciples. Now, His rights of requisition had been taken from
Him. Humans who have no right to lay claim to anything
hardly have strength enough to carry the burden of existence.
The barest necessities were taken from Him — bread and water,
and human companionship. The One through whom everything was created had no rights to any property; even His
clothes were gambled away by greedy soldiers.

Jerusalem, the "city of God's peace," open to every Israelite
in the world, was closed to Him. Like all who suffer human
degradation or uncleanness, who belong to a "lower" status or
have the "wrong" color of skin, Jesus was thrust out of Jerusalem, the city over which He had wept as He uttered the one
backward-looking "If only" He ever spoke, "If you, even you,
had only known on this day what would bring you peace — but
now it is hidden from your eyes" (Luke 19:42).

I never really understood the importance of Hebrews 13:12-
13 until I began preaching the Good News to the Untouchables of India. In the area where we worked, the villages were
the remains of walled ancient towns, built to protect inhabit-
ants from robbers and invaders. The Outcastes, considered to
be reincarnated recipients of divine punishment for their sins
in a former life, ever unclean and contaminating, were forced
to live in a separated, segregated, ghetto-like section called the
keri. Located outside the walls, the keri has its own inferior
well, or no water supply at all, thus requiring the people to
walk great distances to fetch water, often muddy and polluted.
In many ways the keri is the village dump, where not only
garbage but also the carcasses of dead animals are thrown. No
high caste Hindu will enter it except under the direst of
circumstances.

Now you can understand why the words of Hebrews 13:12-
13 came to have special meaning for me and were often used

as a text for my messages in India. "And so Jesus also suffered outside the city gate to make the people holy through His own blood. Let us, then, go to Him outside the camp, bearing the disgrace He bore."

Very often my sermon would be interrupted. "Wait a minute, Sir. Are you telling us that Jesus, this Son of God, was crucified *outside the walls? Died inside the keri? Do you mean He loved us that much?"* The traditional clicking of tongues and other audible expressions of amazement which came from the listeners assured me that a God of love, formerly beyond comprehension, was beginning to be real to them through His deep identification with their plight.

He Descended into Hell

Seven years before the *Titanic* was discovered, *National Geographic* magazine began preparations for the day when the ship would be found and could be photographed. Upon its discovery in 1985, photographer Emory Kristof began gauging water depth and problems of visibility. The descent to a two-and-one-half mile depth required expensive technology. Finally, in 1991, with the help of scientists, filmmakers, and two submarines mounted with motion-picture lights used for the underwater film, *The Abyss,* Kristof made a remarkable series of pictures which appeared in the magazine. The prepublication ad asked, "How far will a *Geographic* photographer go to get the perfect shot?"[3]

How far will God go to reveal His caring love for sinful and suffering humans? Now we know. After centuries of careful preparation through the words of messengers and prophets, the Living Word became flesh and went all the way to the abyss. We marvel at the incredible depths of pain in Christ's cry of dereliction from the cross.

But the final and deepest identification was not that Jesus was despised and rejected by people, and denied and deserted by His disciples. Rather, it was a mysterious and unfathomable experience of being abandoned and forsaken by God Himself.

When He cried out in anguish, "My God, My God, why have You forsaken Me?" there was no answer. The heavens were not only silent but seemed vacant (Mark 15:33-34).

Even the forces of nature added to His solitary emptiness. For the noonday turned into darkness so that Jesus was not able to see His mother, the Apostle John, and a few faithful women who were nearby to comfort Him. Thus Christ experienced *an aspect of hell* He had described in His teachings and parables as being "cast into outer darkness." When we say with the ancient creeds that on the cross "He descended into hell," we are saying that Jesus Christ has entered into every form of fear, terror, and anxiety which we experience at our lowest moments of rejection, abandonment, and depression.

In a lifetime of listening to hurting people, I have heard many personal descents into hell with its abyss of emotional pain. And again and again I have found that the most therapeutic turning point in the healing process is when people discover that God not only knows and cares but also *understands how they feel.*

As I write, the face of one counselee comes to mind. It had been a second marriage for Ashley and her husband, and involved children from both sides. Later they had a child of their own. Things went well for many years until his alcoholism and infidelity shattered her dreams. He finally left and moved in with the other woman. It was in the midst of the divorce and a complicated custody settlement that he became more hateful and seemed to go out of his way to hurt her at every point. The most painful blow came in court when he accused her of not loving one of *his* children, now a teenager. I shall never forget her anguished look and broken tone of voice when she told me how she had taken over that youngster when he was just a toddler, "Dr. Seamands, I loved that kid with all my heart. I quit my job to stay home and care for him. He had been so neglected he was downright emaciated, and my heart went out to him. I literally poured my life and my love into him as if he were my very own. And now to be accused in court of not loving him — oh, I can't tell you how much that hurt me. It felt like a knife in my stomach." Her tears flowed freely with every word. The miracle was that in spite of her deep hurt and anger, she never allowed bitterness or resentment to establish a beachhead in her heart. How was this possible? Because every time we prayed together, we would remind ourselves that our Lord too had been betrayed, abandoned, falsely accused, and had cried out in agony. We knew that He knew how she felt and that every feeling could be unashamedly shared with Him.

> For ours is no High Priest who cannot sympathize with our weaknesses—He Himself has shared fully in all our experience of temptation except that He never sinned. Let us therefore approach the throne of grace with fullest confidence, that we may receive mercy for our failures and grace to help in the hour of need (Hebrews 4:15-16, PH).

From Identification to Action

As Mary and Martha watched Jesus weep, and heard Him groaning within His spirit, their attention was riveted upon Him. By His words and actions, He had guided them on the first two steps of their journey from blame to belief. He had brought them out of the past into the present, and had helped them understand that He fully understood their pain. The Jews who saw Jesus' tears understood their full implication. "See how He loved him!" they exclaimed.

Now Jesus is going to lead the two sisters into taking the next step, one that is very important if they are to "see the glory of God." They will need to hold on to the love they have just witnessed and experienced anew through Jesus' words and actions. But even more, they will need to be held by that love, for this will be the most difficult and painful step in their journey of faith.

"Take away the stone."

John 11:39

5

Letting in the Light

As we follow Jesus' dealings with Martha and Mary, we are struck by a contrast. Until now, we have seen nothing but tenderness and compassion. He has wept, groaned with grief, and completely identified with the pain and sorrow of His friends. But Jesus is also the Wonderful Counselor. True to His name, we will now see the delicate balance between tenderness and toughness, compassion and confrontation.

"Jesus, once more deeply moved, came to the tomb. It was a cave with a stone laid across the entrance. 'Take away the stone,' He said" (John 11:38-39).

There they are in stark contrast, yet strong combination. "Jesus once more deeply moved" with compassion came to the tomb and confronted them with the command, "Take away the stone." Although at first glance, compassion and confrontation seem to be opposites, they actually form the grand paradox at the heart of many incidents in Jesus' ministry.

After healing the man at the pool of Bethesda, Jesus said to him sternly, "See, you are well again. Stop sinning or something worse may happen to you" (John 5:14). To the adulterous woman about to be stoned by the self-righteous crowd, He spoke with great tenderness, "Neither do I condemn you," but immediately added, "Go now and leave your life of sin" (John 8:11). After His sensitive and loving conversation with the woman at the well, He forced her to look at her promiscuous lifestyle with, "The fact is, you have had five husbands, and the man you now have is not your husband" (John 4:18).

In truth, these two characteristics are not opposites at all. Rather, they are both evidences of Christ's love. When Jesus wept, it showed that He cared. And when He confronted, that also showed how much He cared. We pointed out that the Greeks thought God's chief characteristic was *apatheia* or apathy, and therefore He couldn't be touched by our sorrows and pain. But a God who doesn't care enough to comfort us amid our sorrows also doesn't care enough to confront us about our sins.

Tough Love

Although we know that Jesus loved people in general and His disciples in particular, there are only three times we are told that Jesus loved individual persons. Our story is one such reference. Jesus loved Martha, Mary, and Lazarus, the members of His adopted family at Bethany. John, the writer of this Gospel, is often called the "disciple whom Jesus loved" (John 13:23; 21:7, 20). These two, based upon family affection and spiritual affinity, are easier to understand than the third, a person Jesus had never met before. It was the rich young ruler who came inquiring about eternal life. As Mark tells us, "Jesus looked at him and loved him." His youthful appearance, his questing mind, and his spiritual potential drew an immediate and deep affection from Jesus. But how did He express this love? By commending him for all his good qualities? No, by immediately confronting him with what he did not have. "One thing you lack. Go, sell everything you have and give to the poor. . . . Then come, follow Me" (10:21). Jesus loved him enough to listen to him, but loved him too much to just tell him what he would like to hear. He loved him so much that He was even willing to lose him by forcing the young man to face his responsibility.

Brennan Manning speaks of the "relentless tenderness of

Jesus,"¹ and C.S. Lewis often uses a striking phrase borrowed from one of his mentors, George MacDonald, "the inexorable love of God." Jesus' love in action pictures God's love for us. It is a love filled with tenderness and compassion, but also a holy love. For love apart from deep moral concern for the beloved is not true agape-love. Rather, it is sloppy-agape.

It is this kind of tough love which led Jesus, deeply moved with compassion, to come to the tomb and give what seemed to Martha to be the cruel and heartless order to remove the stone from the grave. She naturally protested, and in effect told Jesus they'd better not do that. "But, Lord, by this time there is a bad odor, for he has been there for four days." Jesus certainly knew this when He gave the command, so why did He insist on it? The obvious answer is in order that Lazarus could come out of the tomb.

But as a part of the "sign," the meaning of this step in the sisters' movement toward faith is significant. The stone had to be removed in order to let in the light. Without light there could be no truth or new life. The stone represents the many ways we try to keep things covered up, so we don't have to face the truth or see what the light will reveal. Like Martha, we know this can be a very unpleasant and painful process. I have heard the equivalent of Martha's protest from many troubled, trembling counselees, "I don't want to talk about it. It hurts too much. I'd rather go on trying to forget it. Maybe it's better if we just leave things the way they are. I don't know what might happen if things change."

Light, Life, and Truth

Throughout Scripture, light and life are always connected.

"In Him was life, and that life was the light of men" (John 1:4).

"I am the light of the world. Whoever follows Me will never walk in darkness, but will have the light of life" (John 8:12).

"For you were once darkness, but now you are light in the Lord. Live as children of light" (Ephesians 5:8).

There is also a close connection between light and truth. It is light which enables us to see the truth, respond to it, and then experience new life.

What does the Bible mean by "light"? Fortunately, Paul has given us an excellent, working definition, "Everything exposed by the light becomes visible, for it is light that makes everything visible" (Ephesians 5:13-14). The Phillips translation says it even more clearly, "For light is capable of showing up everything for what it really is." Light, then, is that which reveals or shows things as they really are.

Imagine coming into a strange room at night. It's completely dark and you are trying to reach a light switch. As you grope your way around, you stumble against something. It feels like a table or the corner of a desk. Finally you find the switch. As soon as you turn on the light, you discover it's a large stereo with speakers on either side. Now you know exactly what it is — the light made that possible.

Several experiences in India made me appreciate this biblical definition. Every year we attended a large Christian convention in the middle of a forest. After everyone had retired for the night in their tents and put out their hurricane lanterns, the forest was pitch dark. One night a woman awakened, suffering from a bad headache. Not wanting to disturb the other ladies in her tent, she quietly began feeling around in the tent-pocket nearest her cot until she found what she was searching for, a tube of mentholated salve she had brought back from the States while on a recent furlough. She vigorously rubbed it all over her forehead until its cooling, analgesic properties relieved her headache and she was able to go back to sleep. Imagine her chagrin, and her companions' hilarity, when the morning light revealed that she had smeared a mint-flavored toothpaste all over her forehead!

Another incident at the same encampment wasn't quite as funny. My mother and dad had retired for the night on their camp cots, safely tucked in under their mosquito nets. Mother, a light sleeper, heard a strange sound in the tent. Dad was asleep and protested when she woke him up. "Go back to sleep; it's probably some stray dog looking for scraps left from supper." But Mom insisted until Dad reluctantly shined his big flashlight into the darkness. No, it wasn't a dog; it was a ten-foot python crawling between their cots! You can be sure Dad was wide awake by the time he killed it with the trusty Boy Scout hatchet he kept close by for just such emergencies. Again, it was light that made things visible and revealed the snake for what it really was.

John reminds us, "God is light; in Him there is no darkness at all." So, to "take away the stone" is to live out the admonition, "Walk in the light, as He is in the light" (1 John 1:5, 7). This means to make a conscious decision to not keep any area of life "in the dark." Instead, it is to decide to open ourselves fully to God's light; and if we see something we thought was a harmless dog but turns out to be a dangerous snake, we will ask God to get rid of it.

Stuffing the Truth

Unfortunately I have not always lived up to that high ideal. There have been times when I have deliberately done quite the opposite. During my seminary days, in addition to being a student pastor on weekends, I was the janitor of the married housing unit. I would begin my work early in the morning, which meant that in winter it was still dark. Starting on the top floor and working my way down, I would clean the hallways, bathrooms, and stairs on each level. By the time I had finished the first floor, the sun was shining brightly through a window located at the east end of a long hallway. The bright rays of light revealed traces of dust and dirt which I had missed. Most of the time I went back and cleaned those places over again. But once in a while, when I was overtired, or needed to study for an exam or finish a paper, I just pulled the shade down on that window.

I recently received a letter from a woman who had read one of my books; the Spirit had used it to shine His light into her heart. As is so often the case, the life story she shared was a mixture of both the sins of others and her own. But she had buried it all in the limbo of the forgotten until a midlife tragedy painfully exhumed it. The book generated new hope but also greatly increased her fears. She described years of denial and the refusal to face the truth in this way, "I've been a Stuffer, a terrible Stuffer. I'm just finding out how much has to come out, and I'm not sure I can stand having it pulled out." Her letter reminded me of those days when I was a Puller!

It's not hard to understand Martha's protest. We know why she didn't want to face the decay and despair of what was in that dark grave. Like all of us she was afraid, for when we "take off the lid" we know that not only will the light go in, but the truth will come out. It's the fear of how nasty, smelly, and humiliating that might be which can overwhelm us into keeping the barriers in place, and prevent us from doing what William James described as "exteriorizing the rottenness."[2]

The problem is that in our pain and fear we have forgotten the weeping Christ and His full understanding of what we are feeling, because of His total identification with us on the cross. Unlike Martha, the light to which we open ourselves is the light of the cross. And the light of the cross reveals that where God saw us at our *worst*, He loved us the *most*. If God was going to stop loving us, He would have done it a long time ago, because He saw and felt it all on the cross.

When God shines the cross-beams of His light into the dark caves and graves of our lives, it is not so that He can find out something about us He doesn't already know. It is so that we can find out something about ourselves *we* may not know, or may not even want to know, and so that we can allow His grace and love to enter that hidden, hurting area of our lives. The cross is God's laser light — it exposes, sometimes even sears, but always *in order to heal.*

Therefore, we don't need to be afraid anymore. *We can now face anything because He has already faced everything.* As a former colleague of mine, Dr. Steve Harper, said in a recent sermon, "You can stare your worst sin or greatest failure in the face when you hold the hand of Jesus." And that's true because there are nailprints in His hand, scars that you and I put there when we helped nail Him to the cross. It is this that gives us the courage to take away the stone.

Contemplating the Cross

During my thirty years of counseling at Asbury, I kept the same painting hanging on the wall so that my counselees would face it. It was a large copy of Salvador Dali's *Christ of St. John of the Cross*. It is an unusual portrayal of the Crucifixion. Instead of looking up at the cross from ground level, the painting looks down from above, as if from God's perspective. The cross is massive and seems to loom over the whole world. Jesus is pictured as young and strong and holding back the darkness that surrounds Him. In the foreground, the earth, the sky, and the sea are all lit with the light streaming forth from the cross. It's as if we are seeing the whole world through its light.

During those years there were hundreds of occasions when counselees seemed to reach an impasse. Sometimes it was because of the terrifying memories of abuse, betrayal, abandonment, or rejection, the sins against them which kept them from moving on. Other times it was the heavy burden of guilt and shame from their own sins. Often it was a complex intertwining of both. Whenever we reached that place, I always turned toward the painting and asked the person to join me in focusing attention on it. Sometimes there would be several minutes of silence as we did what the mystics of earlier centuries advised, "Contemplate the cross." I knew that "If only" the meaning and message of that scene would get through to them, things could change, because everything looks different in the light of the cross. For in its light we see most clearly the One whom John described as "full of grace and truth" (John 1:14). And in its light we also see clearly the truth about ourselves and about God's grace for us. In its light the line from "Amazing Grace" becomes true for us, " 'Twas grace that taught my heart to fear, and grace my fears relieved!" Times without number, that sight and that light broke the deadlock, and became the turning point in the process of healing.

If You Only Knew

There are beautiful examples of "If only" in Scripture which represent such turning points. None is more striking than the story of the woman at the well in John 4. To the Christian counselor, Christ's use of surprise, curiosity, listening, indirect and direct questions, along with His unique combination of compassion and confrontation, make it the classic case study of the Wonderful Counselor at His infinite best. However, in this instance, we are more interested in its message than its methods.

Although her life, from a moral and spiritual perspective, is completely different than Martha's, there are some aspects of the Samaritan woman's personality which resemble Martha's. Her rather barbed protest when Jesus requested a drink of water shows that she too was blunt, frank, and spoke her mind freely. She thought she had ended the conversation. But Jesus' reply was like the right bait for the right fish, and she was instantly hooked, "If You only knew." Regardless of age everyone uses that bait to get an interesting conversation started. Little kids say, "Don't you wish you knew?" Teenagers say, "Wouldn't you like to know?" And grown-ups say, "If you only knew." Watch how it worked with this woman, and how beautifully Jesus then led her step by step to the place where she finally believed in Him.

Let us begin by looking at some of the things we know about this woman, and something we don't know. First, there was something everybody knew, that she was a sinful woman. No one in the village said, "If you only knew," because everybody knew all about her. Her reputation was well established as a social outcast, a bad woman. Long before talk shows or "A Current Affair," there was the village well, the gossip center of town. Obviously her current affair was public knowledge. The one good thing about the fact that everybody knew was that later on, when she began witnessing about Jesus, she had no trouble drawing a crowd. Any change in her life would naturally be the talk of the town.

Then there was something about her that only she knew and Jesus knew, but she didn't know that He knew. She thought she was the only one who knew that she wasn't happy. People thought she was, because on the outside she acted happy. After all, she had enjoyed plenty of attention and affection and gifts from so many different men. It seemed like an exciting, glamorous kind of life, but Jesus knew that behind the mask of happiness there was an inner emptiness, an unfilled life, and a deep thirst.

I am grateful that people have trusted me with the privilege of knowing their true selves. So often, as I've heard people make judgments about others based solely on what they can observe on the outside, I've wanted to say, "If you only knew what was really going on inside that person."

● If you only knew about Rick, the rebellious, brash, smart aleck teenager who enjoyed talking about his highly touted exploits. He seemed hardened to spiritual values, flippant, and eager to shock everybody, especially girls.

A lot of religious parents don't understand that teenagers often have no way to rebel against them except by flaunting their opposition to many of the parents' firmly held "convictions." I had to laugh one day when Rick came by and told me he had lost 175 pounds that week. When I looked puzzled he smiled and explained, "I got my hair cut this week and got Dad off my back!" But if you only knew, if you could have heard him tell me of his self-despising, and of how many times he had driven his car at high speeds on a two-lane road, hoping he would "accidentally" kill himself. If you only knew how much hunger for reality was behind that mask of rebellion.

● If you only knew the truth about Sandy. Her skirts were too high, her neckline too low, and her makeup too thick. She was flippant and flirtatious and an easy make for the guys. But if you only knew, after those weekend parties, how she sobbed herself to sleep after battling against an overdose of sleeping pills. If you could only have heard her say, "O Doc, I've given so much of myself away so many times I feel like there's really not much left. If only some decent guy would date me!"

• If you only knew that prim and proper woman in the church. Her Christian life was mostly do's and don'ts and she could be hateful and mean-spirited. People told me she had the fastest tongue in the east and everybody was afraid of it being turned on them. But if you only could have heard her say to me, "Pastor, I don't want to be like this. I know how hateful I can be and I despise myself for it. I love God and want to please Him. What's wrong with me? Why do I act this way?"

• And then there was the judge who came to see me. He had a reputation for being heartless and tough and giving the maximum sentences. But in his fifties he had made a very disturbing discovery. "If I had only known," he said, "there were times I would have been more understanding and shown more mercy." What had shaken him up so much? He said God had shown him that he too was capable of the same kinds of crimes he had punished so severely. The only difference was that his life had never given him the opportunity to do them. I'll never forget his words, "I'm just now discovering my capacity for evil, my potential for sin, and it has really scared me. God has been so good to me and I never realized it." This new awareness had driven him to realize his own need of the Savior.

If we only knew . . . Jesus did know that the Samaritan woman wasn't happy with the kind of life she was living. But there was a third thing in this situation that only Jesus knew. The people didn't know it, the woman didn't know it, but He did . . . that she didn't have to continue living this way. Jesus knew that she could be changed and live a new life . . . if only she would come to know who *she* really was and who *He* really was! The great hymn writer Fanny Crosby was totally blind, but she saw clearly how this kind of transformation could take place, even in the most damaged lives. In one of her best-loved hymns, "Rescue the Perishing," she wrote these perceptive and beautiful words,

Down in the human heart, crushed by the tempter,
Feelings lie buried that grace can restore;
Touched by a loving heart, wakened by kindness,
Chords that were broken will vibrate once more.[3]

How She Came to Know

We all know the wonderful ending of the story. Let me remind
you of how marvelously Jesus led her, step by step, to the place
where she came to know three great life-changing truths: who
Jesus really was, who she really was, and what the Living Water really was.

Her journey of faith is the story of a growing consciousness
and appreciation of this unusual Man at the well. She didn't
even begin from neutral ground but rather started with disre-
spect minus ten. "You are a Jew." John explains that this was
the most prejudicial thing she could say, "For Jews do not
associate with Samaritans" (4:9). After His offer of Living
Water, she moved toward respect, "Sir . . . " she said. But not
until Jesus forced her to take off her mask, let in the light, and
be honest about the kind of sinful life she was living, could she
take the next step. Her estimate of Jesus moved up to a higher
level, "Sir, I see that You are a prophet."

But, she was not quite ready, and like many of us she started
a theological discussion in order to hide her true need of something beyond head knowledge. Jesus accepted her right where
she was and led her to the next rung on the ladder of faith.
This time she used the term "Messiah, Christ." Then Jesus
revealed that He was the Christ, the Source of Living Water,
and she came to know that salvation is a *gift* to be received
from God.

Isn't it interesting how often the Holy Spirit puts these steps
together: discovering who we really are and who Jesus really is.
When we we discover we are *sinners*, then we discover He is
the *Savior* who offers us the free gift of *salvation*. It seemed to
come to her all at once, for when she hurried from the well she
was so excited that she left her waterpot, something no woman
in the East would ever intentionally do. And running back into

town she exclaimed to the people, "Come, see a Man who told me everything I ever did. Could this be the Christ?" Her discovery of who Jesus really was convinced many others as well.

> Many of the Samaritans from that town believed in Him because of the woman's testimony, "He told me everything I ever did." So when the Samaritans came to Him, they urged Him to stay with them, and He stayed two days. And because of His words many more became believers.
> They said to the woman, "We no longer believe just because of what you said; now we have heard for ourselves and we know that this Man really is the Savior of the world (4:39-42).

This is what happens when the light is let in and the truth comes out. Then, and then only, is there possibility of new life. This is why Jesus was so insistent to Martha, and to all of us, "Take away the stone!"

*"But, Lord . . . by this time
there is a bad odor."*

John 11:39

6

Looking into the Grave

W e now need to look into our hearts to see if they contain any of the "If only" patterns of blame which keep us from moving forward on our journey toward belief and new life. In this chapter we will consider the "If onlys" of clinging, longing, and loathing. In chapter 7, we will look at the "If onlys" of excusing, disobeying, and wishful thinking.

John describes the tomb of Lazarus as "a cave with a stone laid across the entrance." So, even after they obeyed Jesus' command and removed the stone to let in the light, the cave would still be partially darkened and shadowy.

As we look into the hidden caverns of our hearts it is helpful to remember these profound words, "If I say, 'Surely the darkness will hide me and the light become night around me,' even the darkness will not be dark to You; the night will shine like the day, for darkness is as light to You" (Psalm 139:11-12).

David began his psalm by telling us that God has already searched us and knows everything about us, even from the moment of conception in our mother's womb (139:1-9, 13-18). In spite of this all-embracing knowledge, which includes some dark things, the cross assures us that God still loves us with a costly, caring love. Therefore, although we may have many fears, we can find the courage to look into the hidden caverns of our hearts and pray with David, "Search me, O God, and know my heart; test me and know my anxious thoughts. See if there is any offensive way in me, and lead me in the way everlasting" (139:23-24). Let us begin our inward search by considering three backward-looking "If onlys" of Scripture.

1. THE IF ONLY OF CLINGING

Early in my ministry a college coed sought counseling for her emotional and spiritual problems. Charlene grew up in an extremely unpredictable and dysfunctional home and experienced many forms of abuse. To make matters worse, these behaviors were mixed with a veneer of legalistic Christianity which, in its own way, was religiously abusive. Her hurts were very deep and so were her hates and her hit-backs. We spent many months in regular counseling sessions and had made steady progress working through her long lists of "If onlys." Charlene carried a great deal of emotional pain—a lot to forgive plus much for which she needed forgiveness.

Finally, the day came when I felt she was ready to make a major decision regarding her willingness to relinquish the past and to begin a new life in Christ. We were seated together in my office and had started a time of prayer. I could sense Charlene's struggle with some very painful memories as she prayed for the grace for forgiveness. Suddenly she stopped, stood up and walked over toward the wall, and began sobbing as she stared out the window. I waited, silently praying for that transforming miracle I had witnessed in so many people. Instead, she turned and said in a tone filled with bitter sadness, "I can't give them up. I'm sorry, but I just can't give up my resentments. *I can't give them up. They're all I've got!*"

She came back to see me again. We counseled some more and, at her request, we tried to pray together. The same thing happened. She returned a third time and once more ended an attempt to pray with those very same words, *"I just can't give them up. They're all I've got!"* After that she never came back to see me again. She graduated that year and I lost contact with her, as she melted into the stream of thousands of students I had known during my ministry at Asbury.

Almost seventeen years later, I preached one Sunday morning in a downtown church in a distant state. After the service
a woman came up and greeted me. She identified herself as
Charlene and asked if I remembered our conversations
together during her college days. When I assured her that I
did, she was quiet for a few moments and then big tears began
to spill down her cheeks. "O Doc," she said with deep feeling,
"two divorces and one nervous breakdown later, I guess I really
should have given them up." And before I had time to respond, she turned and walked away. I haven't seen or heard
from her since!

What had happened to Charlene? Certainly the basic cause
of her ongoing trauma was her refusal to forgive those who had
hurt her so deeply. Again and again Jesus said in no uncertain
terms that our unwillingness to forgive others destroys the
bridge over which God's grace and forgiveness come to us.
"For if you forgive men when they sin against you, your Heavenly Father will also forgive you. But if you do not forgive men
their sins, your Father will not forgive your sins" (Matthew
6:14-15).

But in Charlene's case, the consequences were much deeper
than a refusal to forgive. By clinging to the pains of her past,
the "If onlys" of blame had become the keystone in the arch of
her personality. She had built her life around them so that her
victimization was the basis of her identity. "They're all I've
got" meant, "That's all the identity I have. That's who I am.
At least, it's the only *me* I've ever known. If I give them up, I
don't know who I will be. I'm not sure that I'll even exist. I
know they keep destroying me, but I can't risk losing my very
selfhood. *They are me!*"

Remembering the Pain

Charlene's story illustrates the need for Christ's tender-tough-
ness to which we have already referred. Many of our emotional
and spiritual problems have their origin in unhealthy and destructive experiences which lie buried in the basements of our

personalities. Such incidents often become the soil in which the seeds of damaged emotions are sown. In adulthood, these grow into wrong ways of coping with life in general, and become unhealthy patterns of relating to God, ourselves, and others. It is difficult to simply outgrow these formative experiences, and special counseling and prayer for inner healing are often necessary.

Jesus said some extremely harsh things about those who offend the very young and cause the "little ones" to stumble. The offense worsens when we attempt to hide these dark secrets from the healing light of God's understanding, love, and healing grace. Yet, it is so painful to uncover the hidden recesses of the personality and discover the offensive springs from which flow our emotional discomforts and spiritual deformities. As we look back, we not only remember certain happenings but also reexperience the emotions that surrounded them. Through counseling and recovery, as we relinquish those painful pushes from the past and reframe them in the light of God's purposes, we can learn how to reprogram unhealthy personality patterns. By God's grace we are then on the way to emotional and spiritual wholeness.

At the heart of this procedure, there is often much introspection and retrospection. From a biblical standpoint, "remembrance" or "remembering" is a vital part of conscience that stirs up recognition of need, repentance, renewal, healing, and restoration. As a pastor, I learned that we cannot turn this delicate process into a fixed spiritual system with four laws, three steps, two blessings, or one gift. And as a counselor, I learned that we cannot force it into a predetermined counseling method. Each human has a built-in timetable, and God has His own divine schedule. It is only through careful listening and prayerful discernment that we counselors can learn to be sensitive to both. In all my writings I have stressed that healing contains both the elements of crisis and process.

But in this very course of action, it is essential to maintain a sense of balance and proportion. The Scriptures portray a certain kind of retrospection as an unhealthy and even sinful attitude. There are warnings against the dangerous consequences of a prolonged retrospection, the "If only" of the frozen, backward look which can become a permanent lifestyle.

Perhaps the most interesting Scripture illustration of this is found in Jesus' warning to "Remember Lot's wife" (Luke 17:32), referring back to Genesis 19:15-26. When God was about to destroy Sodom and Gomorrah, He sent special messengers who told Lot, "Flee for your lives! Don't look back, and don't stop anywhere in the plain!" There follows the story of Lot's flight from impending doom, the destruction of the cities, and those fateful words, "But Lot's wife looked back, and she became a pillar of salt."

Building an Identity on Blame

In the healing process there is a time when it is necessary to make the crucial decision to stop looking back and begin looking forward. Otherwise, we too become prisoners of the past, entombed in a pillar of emotional and spiritual salt.[1] Unless we look forward, the original painful and harmful incidents can work themselves into the very process of our growth, and somehow develop a whole life of their own. They become an entire existence which is fed by our imaginations, fertilized by our fears, and fueled by our desires. When that happens, we are no longer dealing with something that has occurred only in the *past*. It is now a real and ongoing part of the *present*, and will most likely be projected into the *future*.

Continued "If onlying," what former generations called "vain regret," no longer has any psychological or spiritual value. Instead, it becomes a vise which grips us more and more firmly, as through the years we become increasingly "set in our ways." Finally, we become our own judges, sentencing ourselves to our own prisons where we are our own jailers. We carry our past around with us like a snail does its shell, impeding our own growth and holding ourselves back from ever reaching our full potential in Christ.

Victimization then becomes the basis of our self-identity,

self-worth, and self-esteem. When we cling to our "If onlys" of blame, we take those occasions where we have been victims of other people's sins and change them from incidents and accidents into the very essence of our character. They are no longer *what happened* to us, but *who we are.*

This gives the past a power over us which the Bible claims it does not have, since Christ "has completely annulled it by nailing it to the cross. And then, having drawn the sting of all the powers and authorities ranged against us, He exposed them, shattered, empty and defeated, in His own triumphant victory! (Colossians 2:14-15, PH)

Therefore, we no longer need to be victims to anyone's sins, ours or others, or let them determine our present identity. We are assured we can be freed from that old identity and can become a "new creation" in Christ (2 Corinthians 5:17). Now, *who* we are is no longer based on *what we did,* or what *others did to us.* It is now based on *whose* we are and *who He considers us to be.* And His Word makes it crystal clear that we are now "called 'children of God' — and that is not just what we are called, but that's what we *are* . . . here and now . . . we *are* God's children" (1 John 3:1-2, PH).

Let me share with you some excerpts from a recent letter which illustrates so beautifully what we have been describing.

> For a long time I have hung onto past hurts and guilts, as a result of a very painful divorce plus a lot of other hurts experienced prior to that. This is my second marriage and both my husband and I have been aware of the need for healing. It has been a gradual process, but the conference was a turning point for both of us. When you asked those in need to stand for prayer we stood together, and we both felt a strong sense of God's healing presence.
>
> Two nights later I had a wonderful dream. Together with a line of people I was approaching a person who put our hands on a block and drove nails into the palms. Then we all walked around, our hands bandaged and hurting. Suddenly Jesus was there and said He would remove the nails whenever we would allow it, and would heal the wounds. But He said that we had to decide when we were ready to let Him do it. I asked Jesus to take out the nails and heal me. Though I was terribly scared it

would hurt a lot, the nails just seemed to float out without any pain, and instantly the wounds were healed.

That was the end of the dream. When I awakened, I realized I had released all my past hurts, and I felt myself opening up and receiving the fullness of His healing grace. God has already begun using us to minister to others in pain.

2. THE IF ONLY OF LONGING

The most familiar biblical illustration of looking backward is the story of the Children of Israel as they grumbled against Moses and Aaron.

> In the desert the whole community grumbled against Moses and Aaron. The Israelites said to them, "If only we had died by the Lord's hand in Egypt! There we sat around pots of meat and ate all the food we wanted, but you have brought us out into this desert to starve this entire assembly to death" (Exodus 16:2-3).

This was just one of several occasions when the Israelites "If onlyed" against their leaders and God. The first time was at the Red Sea when they saw Pharoah's army racing to recapture them (Exodus 14:10-14). The second time was the incident recorded above. And the third time was at Rephidim (Meribah) when they ran short of water (Exodus 17:1-3). As this account is recorded in Numbers 20:3, they said, "If only we had died when our brothers fell dead before the Lord! . . . Why did you bring us up out of Egypt to this terrible place? It has no grain or figs, grapevines or pomegranates. And there is no water to drink."

Centuries later Jeremiah commented on their murmuring against God, in spite of His miraculous deliverances, "But they did not listen or pay attention; instead, they followed the stubborn inclinations of their evil hearts. They went backward and not forward (Jeremiah 7:24).

The If Only of Longing and Lusting

The word *quarrel*, in the sense of murmur or complain, is used twenty times in connection with the Children of Israel, and appears eight times in the Gospels. Paul also reminds us of these ancient incidents and warns, "We should not test the Lord. . . . And do not grumble, as some of them did — and were killed by the destroying angel" (1 Corinthians 10:9-10). Jeremiah's and Paul's comments remind us of Jesus' severe statement to the man who desired to join Him as a disciple, but wanted first to go back home, "No one who puts his hand to the plow and looks back is fit for service in the kingdom of God" (Luke 9:62). The obvious meaning is that a person looking backward is not able to plough a straight furrow. However, Jesus also inferred that the person who *looks* back will most likely *go* back, and end up staying there.

Paul's allegorical interpretation of the Exodus experience leads us toward its psychological truth, for he suggests that it has a significance far beyond the historical setting. "These things which happened to our ancestors are illustrations of the way in which God works, and they were written down to be a warning to us . . . not to crave after evil things as they did. Nor are you to worship false gods as they did" (1 Corinthians 10:11, 6, PH).

This particular form of "If only" is considered by the biblical writers to be very dangerous. When we cease to be thankful and start murmuring, it is easy to begin *longing* and then *lusting*. That is, when we face the trials of our desert experiences, and the necessary disciplines of our discipleship, we may stop praising and then begin desiring to go back to those things from which God has delivered us. This is exactly what the Children of Israel did. When God was leading through their wilderness training course, their memories became selective and they forgot the cruelty of their Egyptian taskmasters, the burning pain of the lash, and the rattle of their chains. They preferred to be well-fed slaves than to face the hardships of a free people. They forgot to be thankful for the special miracles God had performed on their behalf: parting the Red Sea so they could escape Pharaoh's pursuing forces, providing manna and quail for food, and supplying the water from the rock. They forgot God's protecting pillar of cloud by day and His guiding pillar of fire by night. In their forgetfulness of God's divine presence and daily supply, they longed and lusted after a fantasy past. This left them with a complaining "If only" for the present.

Parting with the Past

In counseling Christians, I have found distorted memories to be an ever-present danger. Satan, the ultimate deceiver and "a liar from the beginning," tries to stimulate our memories and paint the walls of the imagination with gaudy murals from our past. He colors them all in unrealistic hues so we fail to remember their emptiness and guilt and destructive consequences. Only the pleasures and "highs" seem to stand out, while the "lows" recede from our memories.

As a youngster, I sometimes played with candles. I would light a candle, let it burn for a while, and then carefully snuff it out. When the column of smoke arose from the candle, I would then try to relight the wick by holding a lighted match in the column. The idea was to see how far up the column and away from the wick I could do this and still relight the candle. It might even be an inch or two.

Toying with a backward look of longing can so quickly relight the fires of desire and passion. This is true in regard to all kinds of sexual immorality, including pornography, voyeurism, and X-rated TV and videos. But it also includes the many misplaced priorities and idols we prefer to call "addictions" or "compulsions," things like food, work, success, gambling, and shopping. The Bible warns us that in this game, Satan usually wins. And so, Paul writes, "Let us have a genuine hatred for evil and a real devotion to good. . . . Don't allow yourselves to be overpowered by evil. Take the offensive — overpower evil with good!" (Romans 12:9, 21, PH)

Praising for the Present

God has given me the great privilege of ministering to future pastors. How often during my years at Asbury a husband or

wife would come for counseling for a particular form of wilderness "If onlying." It was usually one of the older students who
had obeyed the call to preach later in life. Often it was a costly
decision, for it meant leaving a nice home and a good job. And
after the initial joy of transition was over, they often found
themselves in a desert of difficulties which included finances,
housing, loneliness, or the hardships of getting back to studies
after being out of school for years. And their kids reminded
them of how much better the schools were in Ohio. Or their
spouses kept talking about the neighborhood and friends they'd
left back in Kansas. And they both missed whatever the grapes
and pomegranates represented in their lives. Of course, there
was always that ultimate trial of the wilderness life — the
courses in Greek! And before long they would begin "looking
back" and "If onlying."

Now it would be simplistic to overlook the problems of
personality, marriage, or parenting we often had to deal with in
our counseling sessions. But in many instances, the ultimate
cure for the dust and depression of those desert days was to
stop the "If only" of complaining, and begin the practice of
praising once again. And so they would ask God to "restore
the joy of their salvation" and renew their thankful spirits.
When they did this things would begin to change, so that
when they looked back, they remembered how God had miraculously brought them this far, how He had delivered them out
of their empty, midlife American materialism and rescued them
from the slavery of their taskmasters. Because of these remind-
ers, they knew He would continue to provide for their every
need!

Through the years I have become accustomed to the misuse
of Paul's great admonition in Philippians 3:13-14, especially by
those who think counseling is unnecessary. They maintain that
it is wrong to think about the past and its scars, that we do not
need healing for damaged emotions and painful memories, because they are automatically taken care of when we come to
know Christ as Savior. Inevitably, they quote Paul's advice
about "forgetting the past." They overlook the fact that Paul

often wrote with deep feeling about his own past. In fact, the very passage preceding these words is about who he was in the past. It is wrong, even cruel, to use these verses to encourage Christians to *repress* the pains of their past and not seek the healing grace which can come through counseling and prayer.

However, there is a right time and place for Paul's words about putting behind us the things that are past, and one of those is when we discover we have been caught in the grip of this particular kind of "If only." If that be true in your case, then these words are God's counsel for you to follow right now, "One thing I do: forgetting what is behind and straining toward what is ahead, I press on toward the goal to win the prize for which God has called me heavenward in Christ Jesus."

3. THE IF ONLY OF LOATHING

For this "If only," the Bible gives us two examples, not of *saying* but of *doing*. In the one instance, it is the living out of those words in the wrong way, the "If only" of self-loathing which results in self-destruction. In the other, it is the living out of the "If only" in the way of repentance and restoration.

Both Judas and Peter represent the "If only" of looking back at sins and failures. And in both cases, the sins were *very serious*. Judas and Peter both contributed to the sufferings of Jesus, one by *betraying* Him and the other by *denying* Him. They both *disowned* Him, one for the desire for gain, thirty pieces of silver, and the other for fear of loss, people's approval. Furthermore, their sins were irrevocable; there was no way of recalling them, retrieving them, or reversing them.

> The Moving Finger writes; and having writ
> Moves on: nor all thy Piety nor Wit
> Shall lure it back or cancel half a Line,
> Nor all thy Tears wash out a Word of it.[2]

How true these words of Edward Fitzgerald! Although by the time the Gospels were written, Peter was a prominent figure in the church, his denial is one of the few incidents recorded in all four Gospels!

What made the difference in the endings of their stories,

one so tragic and the other so triumphant? Both Peter and Judas were filled with loathing for their sin, and loathing for themselves.

> Immediately a rooster crowed. Then Peter remembered the word Jesus had spoken. . . . And he went outside and wept bitterly. . . .
>
> When Judas, who had betrayed Him, saw that Jesus was condemned, he was seized with remorse and returned the thirty silver coins to the chief priests and the elders. "I have sinned," he said, "for I have betrayed innocent blood."
>
> "What is that to us?" they replied. "That's your responsibility." So Judas threw the money into the temple and left. Then he went away and hanged himself (Matthew 26:75; 27:3-5).

The key to the different endings is in the great distinction between *remorse* and *repentance*. The Greek word for remorse is *metamelomai,* meaning "to feel regret, to be concerned, or in anguish about something." It is a purely backward look which says, "I'm angry at myself for what I did. It was terrible. If only I hadn't done it!" Remorse contains regret, sorrow, and self-hate, but it's all pointed backward.

The Greek word for repentance is *metanoieo.* It has all the backward looking "If only" *feelings* of *metamelomai,* but it also has a forward look which means "to turn around, to make an about-face." The word is sometimes translated, "to change one's mind" or "to be converted." It combines the "If only" of past anguish and self-accusation with the all-important element of *present hope and determination to change direction.* The *King James Version* says, "Judas repented," but this has been rightly corrected in the *New King James Version* to say, "Judas felt remorse."

There is a great message here for some of us who would gladly give thirty or even thirty thousand silver coins to erase some painful memory of sin off the blackboard of our minds. Judas *said* the right thing, "I have sinned!" Those very words are at the heart of what is perhaps the greatest story Jesus ever told. The Prodigal Son, bruised and broken by his own sins, was filled with a kind of self-loathing which only the metaphor of a pigpen could aptly convey to Christ's Jewish listeners.

When he "came to his senses" — what a tremendous phrase — the first thing he said was, "I have sinned." Those words are the turning point of the parable, and they could have been the turning point for Judas. Instead, they turned his self-loathing into self-destruction. The Prodigal was saved because those words turned him around, so that he no longer looked backward or inward or downward. He looked forward to seeing his father and asking him for mercy.

Remorse fills us with regret and self-recrimination. Repentance does too, but it turns us around so that we can see the possibility of being restored to a new relationship. Judas was not lost because he betrayed Jesus, but because he never asked to be forgiven. He self-destructed not because his sin was too great to be forgiven, but because he kept looking back at it and never turned around so that he could look at Jesus once again. He ran not *toward* Jesus but *away* from Him.

Peter, knowing that he too had sinned, "went out and wept bitterly." Of course, there was the great divine initiative; there had to be, since true repentance is always a gift from God (2 Corinthians 7:10). Our responsibility is in deciding whether we will *receive* or *reject* it. The Gospels give us the details of that initiative of grace. Luke tells us, "The Lord turned and looked straight at Peter. Then Peter remembered. . . . And he went outside and wept bitterly" (22:61-62). Mark reminds us that after the Resurrection, the angels sent a special message to Peter, "Go, tell His disciples and Peter" (16:7). And Paul informs us that "Jesus appeared to Peter" (1 Corinthians 15:5). At least Peter was there to receive these wonderful gifts. In his self-loathing, he hadn't run away and destroyed himself. He was available to the offers of God's grace.

There are people today who desperately need this message, for the "If only" of self-loathing is keeping them entombed in a dark cave of guilt and condemnation. They need to break out of their condition by fully accepting God's offer of forgiveness and His offer of grace and courage to forgive themselves. God's grace and self-forgiveness are so closely linked together that without the latter we really do not experience the joy of the former.

Some years back, at the request of a member of my church, I visited a woman in the Intensive Care Unit of the hospital. When I introduced myself she said, "Reverend, I've been trying to pray, but it's no use. I don't know the Bible, and I've not been to church in thirty years. I know God won't listen to me. I've just been too bad." I asked her if she wanted to tell me about it. She requested that I lean closer and then told me a sad and sordid story. When she was a teenager her mother, whom she loved deeply, suddenly died. She was overwhelmed with grief, and the night after the funeral she and her older brother went out and got "roaring drunk." With great shame she then whispered to me how in their drunken stupor they had slept together. After that, life had been downhill all the way. "That's why it's no use for me to pray. I know God can't forgive me, since I sure can't forgive myself."

That very morning Helen and I had read for our devotions from 2 Corinthians 5:19-20. It was fresh in my memory that I was God's personal ambassador with His authority. I took her by the hand and said, "Rosie, my name is David. And I want you to know that God Himself personally sent me to tell you that Jesus died on the cross for you, and that He forgives you for that sin and all the rest of your sins." We talked a little longer and prayed together. Her last words to me were, "What you said God told you to tell me was wonderful. I'm going to try and believe it."

I returned the next morning to see Rosie, but her bed was empty. The nurse recognized me and said, "She died in the night. But she told me to give you a message. 'Tell that Reverend David that I *did* pray, and I *did* believe what God told me, and I've got peace in my heart, and everything between me and God is all right!' "

Second Corinthians 5:19 says, "God was reconciling the world to Himself in Christ, not counting men's sins against them." But I like Rosie's translation, "I believed . . . and everything between me and God is all right!"

"... he has been there four days."

John 11:39

7

Shadows in the Darkness

We are continuing to peer into the darkness of the grave, attempting to find "truth in the inward parts." It is like exploring a cave which was once inhabited by an ancient tribe. When we first enter with a lantern, we see only the largest, most prominent objects. But as our vision adjusts to the darkness, the shadows become realities and we can discern their details. We discover there is more in the cave than we first thought. And the further we allow the light to penetrate, the greater our discoveries. Truly the light is "showing up everything for what it really is." And so we join Paul in his prayer, that the eyes of our hearts may be enlightened (Ephesians 1:18). And then we turn to three more "If onlys" of blame that may be hindering our journey on "the way everlasting."

4. THE IF ONLY OF EXCUSING

This "If only" is best illustrated by the story of the man at the pool of Bethesda.

> Some time later, Jesus went up to Jerusalem for a feast of the Jews. Now there is in Jerusalem near the Sheep Gate a pool, which in Aramaic is called Bethesda, and which is surrounded by five covered colonnades. Here a great number of disabled people used to lie—the blind, the lame, the paralyzed. One who was there had been an invalid for thirty-eight years. When

Jesus saw him lying there and learned that he had been in this
condition for a long time, He asked him, "Do you want to get
well?"

"Sir," the invalid replied, "I have no one to help me into the
pool when the water is stirred. While I am trying to get in,
someone else goes down ahead of me."

Then Jesus said to him, "Get up! Pick up your mat and
walk." At once the man was cured; he picked up his mat and
walked (John 5:1-3, 5-9; see verse 4 in the footnotes or
margin).

In 1888, archeological excavations near the Church of St.
Anne, close to the Sheep Gate of Jerusalem, unearthed five
arched porches and steps leading down into an underground
pool, much like the setting John has described for us. Nowadays we would consider it a warm mineral spring which bubbles
up periodically and has healing properties. But in those days, it
was believed that an angel came down to disturb the waters,
and those who entered the pool at that time were healed. It is
interesting to note that the archeologists also found a faded
fresco on one of the walls depicting an angel and water, con-
firming the ancient tradition. John informs us that among the
collection of human derelicts gathered around the pool was
one "who had been an invalid for thirty-eight years."

Let that time span really sink in. Compare it, for example, to
the length of your life. Or, think of all the events that have
taken place during the past thirty-eight years. Imagine a man
crippled for that length of time. And though we don't know
how long he had actually been at the pool, we are plainly told
it was for "a long time." Surrounded by scores of depressed
cripples, discouraged by unsuccessful attempts to drag himself
down the steps into the pool, and long since abandoned by
family and friends, he simply lay on a lightly padded mat — the
sleeping pallet of that day. It's hard to even imagine how
interminably long each day would seem under those circumstances.

John goes out of his way to inform us that Jesus knew how
long the man had been there. That's why it's even harder to
understand why it was to a *man in that condition* for *that length*

of time that Jesus put His question, "Do you *want* to get well?" Our immediate response is shocked disbelief! Jesus' final statement to him, "See, you are well again. Stop sinning or something worse may happen to you" (v. 14), makes clear that his physical disability was due to a moral malady. Even so, it was completely unlike our Lord to ever say anything to physical, emotional, or spiritual cripples which would increase their sense of hopelessness and condemnation. To such persons He always spoke words of encouragement and hope. So at first glance, it seems quite out of character for Jesus to ask him such a seemingly heartless question.

However, by the man's answer we see that it was neither heartless nor cruel. For this probing question contains two crucial principles which have a direct bearing on our subject. The first is in regard to the *purity of our desires.* Jesus knew that regardless of what we may tell others, we can deceive ourselves as to what we really want. The second is the *responsibility of our choices.* This means that whatever the circumstances, we still have a measure of responsibility, literally response-ability, the ability to choose how we will respond to whatever has happened to us. Together they mean that what happens *in us* is more important than what happens *to us.* We are not able to choose the latter, but we can always choose the former.

But this man's initial response does not assume any such responsibility for himself. Quite the opposite, he even avoids answering Jesus' relentless question by asserting his victimhood. In effect he says, "You don't understand. Of course, I want to get well, but I can't, for no one helps me get into the pool when the angel stirs it up. And even if I do finally drag myself there, it's already full of people and there's no room for me."

John told us us there were five arched porches or colonnades surrounding the pool. They are symbolic of his five big "If onlys," and it looks as if he tried to hide under each one of them.

- *If only* someone cared enough — "Sir, I have no one."
- *If only* someone would help me — "To put me in the pool."

- *If only* I were as strong as the others — "Someone else goes down ahead of me."
- *If only* I hadn't missed the opportunity — "When the water is stirred."
- *If only* I had a chance — "While I am trying."

Everything he said was true. His was a chronic condition, and his very disability made it unlikely that he would be among the first in the pool after the waters were disturbed. But at this point we need to remember a deep psychological observation which only John makes about Jesus, "He did not need anyone to tell Him what people were like: He understood human nature" (2:25, PH). Jesus perceived something about the cripple that went much deeper than his present wretched circumstances.

There are several possible ways to interpret Christ's question. Perhaps the man had been there so long and failed so often that he had not only lost hope, but had also lost much of *a genuine desire* to be healed. In this case Jesus was asking him, "Are you *still* hoping someday you will be healed?"

Or, could it be that a hidden, unresolved sense of guilt for his moral failures made him feel he didn't deserve anything better and needed to continue suffering as a kind of self-atonement for his sins?

Or, was it a combination of several factors so that he had finally come to the place where he accepted his condition as permanent? Deep within his heart of hearts, he might have grown content to remain an invalid, dependent on the alms of the generous.

Dr. Paul Brand, the world-renowned medical missionary, who worked for years restoring the deformed hands of leprosy patients in India, discovered this to be a major problem. He tells of his shock when his earliest prize patient, whose reconstructed hands now looked and performed normally, returned despondent after a few months. He was grateful for his new hands but then went on to complain, "But, Doctor, they're bad *begging* hands. People don't give as generously now." By freeing his fingers from the characteristic "leper's claw," the surgeon had jeopardized the man's main source of income. Dr. Brand's comment in this regard is significant, "The task of restoring dignity to a broken spirit—that is the true meaning of rehabilitation."[1]

This may have been a part of the root problem of the man at the pool. After all, if he were cured, he would then have to accept responsibility for making a living. In this instance, then, Jesus' question could be interpreted as asking, "Do you *really want* to be healed?"

Susan's Sabotaging Sicknesses

I recall a young mother with a long string of physical and emotional problems who came seeking help. She would always take the first ten minutes of our time for an "organ recital," a summary description of her widely assorted aches and pains. She also seemed to catch every virus that came along. This interfered with her ability to work and participate in church and community affairs, and prevented her from establishing fulfilling relationships with her neighbors. She had been a frail, sickly youngster and she remembered her family, friends, teachers, and pastors often saying, "Be careful, Susan; don't overdo it. Remember, you've never really been a very strong person." Those destructive "You are" messages had reinforced her physical weaknesses and had gradually internalized into a debilitating "I am" mind-set.

We began to discover a pattern: illness often came on whenever she was facing extra responsibilities. This kept her in a vicious cycle: the illnesses and ailments gave her respectable excuses to cop out, which in turn made her angry at herself and, as she later came to realize, angry at God for expecting her to do things she was not able to do. Life seemed unfair. She would have liked to participate in community and church events "if only" she were well enough.

The turning point in her healing came when she saw herself in the John 5 story. Jesus' searching question forced her to face a painful reality: despite her protests, she was actually sabotaging her own wellness. Later, when she came to see a whole new picture of God's unconditional grace, she declared, "I was free to fail, so I didn't need any more excuses!" Her recovery continued as she took on more and more responsibilities in "bite-sized pieces," growing stronger in both confidence and competence.

Whatever the hidden agenda Jesus had perceived which led Him to ask such a penetrating question, the sick man's answer confirms that there was one. Jesus' shocking query was intended to cut through his excuses and free him from the self-defeating patterns of blame which would prevent him from receiving the gift of healing.

Jesus' Impossible Command

Without further conversation, Christ gave him an impossible command which seems every bit as heartless and cruel as His question. Now he could have retorted with a kind of defensive resentment, saying that was the very thing he could not do. He could have fallen back on his original arguments and kept lying on his mat. But he didn't, and *that very fact is the beginning of the miracle.*

The great Bible scholar G. Campbell Morgan tells us that at this point we have to depend not on the literal facts of the story but on the facts of the personality of our Lord Himself.[2] For even though Christ was a total stranger to the man, there was something in the look of His eyes and the tone of His voice that stirred him even more than any angelically stirred-up waters could have possibly done. Jesus' question and command were meant not only to refine his desires and revive his hopes, but also to *redirect* them from the *pool* to the *Person*, from troubled waters to the One who is the Source of Living Water. Jesus in effect was saying, "Stop worrying about getting into the pool; stop looking for a particular method or a special time, and look at Me. You are not alone, you do have some-one, not just to help get you into the pool but to heal you. "Get up! Pick up your mat and walk." And some deeply buried spark of hope revived, which in turn fanned his ambivalent motives into a focused flame of genuine desire. A willingness to exercise his response-ability was reborn. Somehow he made the choice to respond, to "trust and obey."

When his will responded, his body was re-created, and his weakened, atrophied muscles restored. The impossible was made possible, and "At once the man was cured; he picked up his mat and walked" (John 5:8-9). Isaiah had prophesied that in the day of the Messiah the lame would "leap like a deer," and the burning sand would "become a pool, the thirsty ground bubbling springs" (Isaiah 35:6-7).

On a recent TV Special called, "The Blame Game: Are We a Nation of Victims?" (ABC, October 26, 1994) John Stossel interviewed a young African-American who was deeply disturbed that so many of his own people continued to blame all their problems on the fact that they are "victims of racism." He told his own story, how he finally broke out of a destructive, inner-city background and became a successful businessman. The turning point was when he stopped playing the blame game and took responsibility for his own choices. When asked how he had been able to do this, he gave this brief but incisive answer, *"The right belief empowers!"*

For the man at the pool, it was the *right belief* in the *right Person.* This is at the very center of the biblical attitude toward moving out of blame to belief. When contact is made between Christ's will for us and our will, expressed in risking obedience to Him, it's like turning on an electrical switch. We plug into a whole new enabling power. The crippled man not only got up and walked but also carried his mat. Because it was the Sabbath, he was breaking the Jewish law (John 5:10-11). It seems ridiculous, but that was what actually caused all the commotion which followed his healing. What a tragedy! The religious critics concentrated on the mat and missed the miracle. If they had understood what was happening, they might have been excited. For he was now carrying the mat that had carried him for thirty-eight years! What a powerful picture of a change from *victim* to *victor.*

The Question behind All Questions

When I find myself in counseling situations where people have "been in this condition for a long time," I tenderly ask a tough question similar to the one Jesus asked the man at the pool. Years ago, I used to ask it too directly by simply inquiring, "Why do you hold onto your past the way you do?" Then I began to realize that many people did not know the answer. When I asked too directly, I simply aroused their defenses and blocked the Holy Spirit from working. I finally learned to phrase the question in a way better suited to help the Spirit melt resistance and enable them to discover the answer themselves. I now say something like this: "I want to ask you a question. Please don't try to answer it too quickly. Take all the time you need. Or, if it will help, take it home with you and think about it as long as you feel it's necessary. Here is the question: 'What need within you is being filled which might make you want to hold onto your past and its pains?'"

In addition to responses which have revealed blame, excuses, and respectable reasons for possible failure, other answers have surprised, even amazed me.

"It makes me feel *special*."

"Without it I would just be an *ordinary* person."

"It offers me *power* over that person."

"It gives me a coverup from facing my *real* problems."

"What would I be without it?"

These and scores of others reveal root reasons why some people will hold onto the pain of their past, in spite of the continued cost of emotional suffering, spiritual defeat, marital failure, and sometimes even physical illness.

This clinging to excuses may or may not be conscious or intentional, but it certainly is tenacious. These folks find it easier to claim victim status and then play the "If only" blame game. We've all heard the old adage, "No pain, no gain." These people seem to go even further, "Unrelinquished pain, greater gain."

Obviously, their settings and situations are totally different from the man at the pool of Bethesda. But some of us, because we've been in our condition for "a long time," feel about as crippled and helpless as he did. We need to listen to Christ's voice, as if His penetrating question were being addressed to us personally, "Do you *really* want to be healed?" If we answer it with ruthless moral honesty, this can be the beginning of our healing.

5. THE IF ONLY OF DISOBEYING

We find another "If only" in the very strange story of a very strange man. His name is Balaam and we learn about him in Numbers 22 to 24. Balaam was a Midianite who lived in the city of Mesopotamia. He had such a reputation as a prophet that before King Balak of Moab went into battle against Israel, he offered Balaam money if he would "curse" Israel, so that Moab would win the war. But Balaam was frightened, so he invited Balak's emissaries to spend the night with him, because he wanted to pray about what he should do.

That night, while he was praying, a clear message came from God, "You must not put a curse on those people, because they are blessed." When King Balak received this reply he wouldn't give up easily, and so he sent the messengers back, raising the amount of his reward. Balaam once again refused, saying, "Even if Balak gave me his palace filled with silver and gold, I could not do anything great or small to go beyond the command of the Lord my God." It sounded like a very pious "If," but he then added a dangerous proviso, "Now stay here tonight . . . and I will find out what else the Lord will tell me" (Numbers 22:12-18).

Balaam had deceived himself, as many of us have done, and he seemed to think maybe God would allow it. In the morning he mounted his donkey and started to ride along with the envoys who were returning to King Balak. This is when the famous incident of Balaam and his talking donkey took place! For God, who was angry about all this, sent an angel armed with a sword to stand in the road, in order to stop Baalam from going farther. Spiritually blinded by his attitude, Balaam was unable see the angel, but the donkey did. After three futile attempts to force the animal to go on, God spoke through the donkey. This opened Balaam's eyes so that he saw the armed angel and perceived him as God's messenger to bar the way. Balaam bowed before him and said, "I have sinned. I did not realize you were standing in the road to oppose me. Now if you are displeased, I will go back" (22:34). In effect Balaam said, "If only I had known this was wrong and displeasing to you, I would not have done it." But God had already told him very plainly not to do it.

"Iffing" versus Obeying

Here we see the "If only" of disobedient compromise. Balaam is one of those people who try to carry water on both shoulders or, in Jesus' words, to "serve two masters." Balaam wanted to share in the destiny of God's people *and* God's enemies. He would have liked to please God, but he also wanted to allow the possibility of pleasing those who opposed God. The rest of the story is mixed, for although Balaam then prophesied several important oracles and even prayed to die the death of the righteous (23:10), his later compromises hastened the moral downfall of many in Israel; he finally died in disgrace, slain along with God's enemies (31:8).

It is indeed a strange story about a strange person, but few of us are complete strangers to its lesson. For many of us have attached some big "If onlys" to our Christian convictions. How often God has made something perfectly clear to us in His Word, or through one of His messengers, and we know what is right and wrong. But we argue or rationalize or, like Balaam, we even say we want to pray about it more. I am not referring to the many issues about which God's people can have sincere differences of opinion. To dogmatize about such matters is to fall into legalism and pharisaism. But there are some absolutes about which God has given clear directions, and we do not need to *argue* or *pray* or *research* to find some "If only" about them.

This reminds me of an occasion when my minister father-in-law, Dr. Warner P. Davis, was receiving a young teenager into the church. He was asking him to take the vows for membership. Among the questions to be asked and the vows taken was one which said, "Will you renounce the devil and all his works?" Trying to be helpful, Dr. Davis said to the youngster, "Say, 'I will,' if you will." To which the boy answered very solemnly, "I will if you will!"

There are many of us who need to stop "If onlying" and start obeying. Too often we have said, "I would have 'If only' you had," when we should have said, "Since you have, I will."

If Only God Would Do Something Spectacular!

There is another aspect to the "If onlying" of disobedience to which Jesus alluded in one of His stories. It's about an unnamed rich man living in extravagant luxury, who failed to care for a poor beggar named Lazarus who sat just outside his gate. When both men died, their status was reversed: the poor beggar went to heaven—"Abraham's bosom"—while the rich man went to hell where he was in great torment. The rich man asked for mercy but was told by Father Abraham that an uncrossable chasm prevented him from doing anything for him. The rich man begged then on behalf of his five brothers, "Send Lazarus to my father's house. . . . Let him warn them, so that they will not also come to this place of torment. . . . If someone from the dead goes to them, they will repent." But Abraham gave this significant reply, "If they do not listen to Moses and the Prophets, they will not be convinced even if someone rises from the dead" (Luke 16:19-31).

If we use this parable as a basis for describing either heaven or hell, we miss the profound truth Jesus is trying to teach us: If we fail to walk in the light God has already given us, and do not respond in obedience to the obvious "duty that lies nearest us," we lose our spiritual capacity to receive more light from Him. Note the "Ifs" in the last two verses:

If someone from the dead goes to them, they will repent.

If they do not listen to Moses and the Prophets ...

The rich man didn't need any special word from God to know that he ought to have provided food and care for a nearby beggar covered with ulcers. His own religious beliefs were crystal clear on that.

Jesus is telling us that if we don't walk in the light of a candle God shines on our way, then it is unlikely we will respond to some bright spotlight He shines on our way. Many of us are waiting for God to do the unusual, the extraordinary, and we say, "If only He would do something like that for me, then I would believe." Jesus repeatedly stressed that the religious leaders of His day were rejecting Him because they had already rejected what the law and the prophets were trying to teach. If they had followed the light of those prior revelations, they would have accepted the Light of the World when He came. "But do not think I will accuse you before the Father. Your accuser is Moses, on whom your hopes are set. If you believed Moses, you would believe Me, for he wrote about Me. But since you do not believe what he wrote, how are you going to believe what I say?" (John 5:45-47)

I have found this spiritual principle to be of great importance in emotional and spiritual healing. I believe it is one of the moral laws God has built into the structure of life — this law of diminishing moral capacity to respond to *big* things, resulting from our failure to obey in *little* things. Care and faithfulness in minor matters is very important for those on the road to wholeness. So is obedience to the daily checkings of the Spirit in seemingly insignificant areas. For it is in those places where He is breaking our bad habits, changing our wrong means of coping, and trying to transform our unhealthy ways of relating to people. When God is reconstructing our broken lives and restoring us to the image of Christ, we make a mistake to say, "No big deal," or "That's just a little thing," or "I'll wait until something big comes along." The important thing is not the size of the issue, but the depth of our willingness to obey. Often the "little things" reveal our last foothold of resistance. We are really saying to ourselves, "It's not much, *but it's mine!"* Yet, Jesus must be Lord of all, if He is to be Lord at all!

In my counseling ministry I have found this to be one of the ways some people evade responsibility and blame God with an "If only." They keep waiting for more and more spectacular revelations ("signs and wonders") before they obey, when they haven't responded to His more quiet, daily directives. Then they excuse themselves with, "I wasn't really sure. If only God had made it plainer, I would have."

Some Bible scholars think Jesus was referring to the raising of Lazarus, since that's the name he gave to the beggar in His parable. Or, perhaps He was hinting at His own forthcoming resurrection, when He would be the One who would rise from the dead. Whatever the case, there were many in Jesus' time who still didn't believe, in spite of such extraordinary evidence. Even that much light didn't convince them, but rather blinded them, because they hadn't walked by the light God had already sent their way to prepare them for the Light of the World.

However, let us thank God that this moral principle also works in a positive direction. "If only" we walk obediently by the lesser lights He provides, then He will grant us bigger and brighter lights to walk by. In the Book of Proverbs, we find God's promise about our *pathway.* "The path of the righteous is like the first gleam of dawn, shining ever brighter till the full light of day" (Proverbs 4:18). When we walk on an increasingly brightening path, then "we, who with unveiled faces all reflect the Lord's glory, are being transformed into His likeness with ever-increasing glory" (2 Corinthians 3:18).

And, when we are faithful in the less important matters, He will make us rulers over the more important ones (Matthew 25:21, 23).

There is one Christian woman who is known throughout the world for her remarkable ministry. On the front cover of *Time,* Mother Teresa was called one of today's "Living Saints" (December 29, 1975). It was her self-sacrificial life that shattered the defenses of Malcolm Muggeridge's cynical paganism, and brought about his surrender to Christ.

At an early age Mother Teresa became a nun and worked as a teacher in a parochial school in Calcutta, where she later became the principal. Most of her pupils were from comfortable homes, but the school was located close to one of Calcutta's worst slums, and God began to stir her heart with compassion for its poor. One day in September 1946, while riding on a train, she heard what she said was a clear call from God. A "call within a call," she described it, since she was already in God's service. In spite of opposition and misunderstanding from church leaders, she finally began the work of caring for the homeless and dying. Within a few years, hundreds of volunteers had joined her; there are now branches worldwide.

In a television special on her life, she told how the work began. It started one day when she felt led to pick up a dying woman lying on the sidewalk, one whose feet were half chewed away by rats and whose wounds were alive with maggots. The interviewer, deeply impressed by the growth of her work, said he had heard that she and her coworkers had picked up and ministered to over 42,000 unwanted and dying people. She replied simply, "Yes, but if I hadn't picked up the *first* body back in 1946, we would never have picked up the other 42,000!" The world is grateful that Mother Teresa answered that first call by obeying and not "If onlying."

6. THE IF ONLY OF WISHFUL THINKING

Let me refresh your mind on the context of this "If only." Absalom was David's third and most favorite son. Without doubt he was the most handsome, the most brilliant, and certainly the most selfish and spoiled of all David's children. And, as is often the case in such instances, Absalom had turned against the father who had spoiled him and finally led a rebellion against him as king. There was a great battle, and as Absalom fled on his donkey through the forest, his long hair got caught in the lower branches of a tree. His donkey ran on and he was left hanging there, unable to free himself.

Along came Joab, commander-in-chief of King David's army. Sizing up the situation, he immediately killed Absalom who was the root cause and leader of the rebellion. When the news of Absalom's death reached David, he "was shaken. He went up to the room over the gateway and wept. As he went, he said, 'O my son Absalom! My son, my son Absalom! If only I had died instead of you—O Absalom, my son, my son!'" (2 Samuel 18:33)

We can certainly understand his deep grief, the lament of a father who has lost his son. But there is another aspect which makes this the perfect illustration of unrealistic "If only" thinking. For David had forgotten he was still the king of the land; he had forgotten the treachery of Absalom, and that thousands of his men had risked their lives and some had died to save the king and the kingdom. So when the people came together to celebrate the victory, David was hysterically mourning, "O Absalom! If only I had died instead of you."

Once again it was the stalwart and sensible Joab whom God used to save the situation. He bravely confronted David and through a bitingly sarcastic speech forced him to face the precarious situation. Long before psychologist William Glasser created the term, Joab used "Reality Therapy." This snapped David out of his weak "If onlying" and brought him back from a world of emotional fantasy into the real world of decisive action. This was what saved the kingdom!

Scott Peck, in his bestseller, *The Road Less Traveled*, says this, "The attempt to avoid legitimate suffering lies at the root of all emotional illness."[3] While I cannot agree with the "all" in his statement, from many years of *living with myself* and *listening to my counselees*, I have come to the conclusion that a basic cause of many emotional and spiritual problems is an *inability to face reality*.

The If Onlys of Romantic Relationships

This inability to face reality is particularly true in romantic involvements. If we look honestly into the cave of our past, most of us will find the remains of some relationship, wrapped in the graveclothes of unrealistic and wishful thinking.

Consider, for instance, the area of courtship. The American system of courtship, the so-called "dating game," can be a risky and cruel business, even for Christians. In spite of all the biblical admonitions against marrying unbelievers or having premarital sex, and despite the many excellent books on the subject and the expert premarital counseling available, dating is filled with wishful "If onlying" and often ends in unhappiness and divorce.

I will always remember one night when I was going over the results of the Taylor-Johnson Temperament Analysis with an engaged couple. Although the test revealed that he had major problems with hostility and anger, he kept denying it. I asked her if she had noticed any symptoms of this. She pointed out a few occasions, but he still denied it and insisted his anger had all been taken care of when he became a Christian. I held on like a bulldog, until finally he said, "Well, I've never told her about it, but I grew up a street kid in the city and got into a lot of trouble fighting with other teenagers." As a result the wedding was postponed; when he wouldn't get help, she broke off their relationship. I still get thank-you notes from this grateful woman who gave up her unrealistic wishes for the future.

The same unreality exists in some marriages as well. Do you remember the famous ad for V-8 juice? Someone would be shown who had just finished a popular soft drink. Then he would taste a V-8, and exclaim, "Wow, I could'a had a V-8!" It was a very successful ad that increased sales considerably. What it really said was, "If only I had drunk a V-8 instead of. . . ." Many a marriage has been made unhappy or even destroyed by such an "If only." "If only I had married So and So!"

An unhappy wife once came to counsel with me. After we talked together for some time she said, "I think I understand what's wrong. We've been married for almost seven years, but I've never really unpacked my bags." I thought she meant they had moved around a lot. "Oh, no," she explained. "I mean that I've never really unpacked my emotional and spiritual bags, never really settled my commitment to this man as my husband. I keep remembering all the guys who dated me in college, and thinking I should have married one of them. My husband is a wonderful man and I haven't been fair to him. I need to stop my wishful thinking and with God's help settle down to make this a good marriage."

You may remember the story of the young medical students in training. One week the interns were making the rounds with a doctor through the Psych Ward. Before they entered one room the doctor explained, "This patient is a classic case of existential or situational depression. Nothing chemical, no disease of the brain. He was engaged to be married to a very beautiful girl. Three weeks before the wedding she fell in love with another guy, ran off, and married him. He just couldn't take it. He fell into a depression and has been here for quite a while. But he's improving and will be okay." The interns observed the patient and took careful notes.

Farther down the hall the doctor again instructed them, "Now this patient is another example of depression from stress, but he's really depressed. I mean, he's so incapacitated he can hardly get out of bed."

One of the interns asked, "What happened to him? Did he lose his fiancée at the last minute too?"

"Oh, no," the doctor replied. "He's the fellow who got the other guy's girl!"

At the other end of the scale are those situations where wishful thinking hangs onto relationships that have no future. As a veteran pastor, I've watched men and women live in a dream world. I've seen singles cling to someone who gave them false hopes about marriage. I've watched them live on bits and pieces that were thrown their way: a rare phone call, a card at Christmas, or an occasional letter. They've built their lives on unrealistic fantasies and let the years slip by, sometimes missing other persons God had for them. Or missing opportunities for happiness in serving where God could use them.

And then, there are also some people whose unrealistic "If onlys" include impossible marriages. I have seen situations when our prayers needed to be for godly courage to face the reality of a necessary divorce. My own view follows that of some of the Reformers who said that marriage was an indissoluble union *except by death or its equivalent.* There are equivalents to death in some marriages, things like continued infidelity, desertion by the unbelieving spouse, physical violence, and sexual abuse. And sometimes God can bring new life even out of the death of a marriage by the possibility of a spiritually based remarriage or a life of fulfillment as a single person. Some married people have been truly victimized and it is wrong for us as individuals and churches to live on unrealistic "If onlys" and fail to help such victims become victors.

Along with Martha and Mary we have come a long way on our spiritual journey. We have taken away the stone, let in the light and, in spite of the pain and stench of the tomb, have had the courage to face the truth about our offensive "If onlys." As God's Spirit has faithfully revealed the truth about the dark areas of our lives, the Light has shown them to be what they really are—ways of excusing ourselves and blaming God and others for our failures. Thank God we have seen the truth, for Jesus tells us that truth sets us free. But then He adds, "If the Son sets you free, you will be free indeed" (John 8:32, 36). We will now join Jesus, the Son, as He challenges us to turn from blame to belief.

"Did I not tell you that if you believed, you would see the glory of God?"

John 11:40

8

The Ifs
of Belief

Jesus has been leading Martha and Mary to bring them to a crucial point. His seemingly senseless delay in not coming as soon as He received their urgent message; His attempt to jolt them out of the past into the present by His "I AM" teachings, which broke open their closed minds so they could at least allow for a new possibility; His weeping which identified with their sorrow; right up to His apparently cruel command to open up the grave, in spite of its offensive odor. All these were necessary steps to prepare them for the battle to believe, in the face of what seemed a hopeless and impossible situation.

The divine-human division of labor stands out so clearly in this story. John puts it this way, "So they took away the stone. Then Jesus looked up and said." The human responsibility was to obey the Master, to take away the stone, to let the darkness and the stench out, and to have the courage to look in. After they looked in, *then* Jesus looked up and began to pray. The answer to many of our our "If onlys" of blaming — of clinging, longing, loathing, excusing, disobeying and wishful thinking — is the "If" of obedient, believing prayer.

A common saying might well be the motto of many of the backward-looking "If onlys" we have been describing. That is, "Seeing is believing." But Jesus reversed this into "Believing is seeing." He said, "If you will believe, you will see the glory of

God!" This is how faith is defined in that great Faith Hall of Fame chapter, Hebrews 11, "Faith is being sure of what we hope for and certain of what we do not see" (11:1). "Blessed are those," said Jesus, "who have not seen and yet have believed" (John 20:29). Yes, to Jesus, "Believing is seeing."

It was in this believing spirit that He looked up and began to pray, " 'Father, I thank You that you have heard Me. I knew that You always hear Me, but I said this for the benefit of the people standing here, that they may believe that You sent Me.' When He had said this, Jesus called in a loud voice, 'Lazarus, come out!' " (John 11:41-43)

The Place and Pattern of Prayer

We can learn much from Jesus' prayer.

• First, there is the simple fact that He prayed. Facing the fearful sight and the foul smell of an open tomb, Jesus prayed. Do we? In the face of all our fearful and offensive "If onlys," our hurts and humiliations, our defeats and disillusionments, our emotional illnesses and our spiritual ailments, have we prayed? Facing the sights and insights God has graciously revealed to us through the light from the books and the sermons and the counselors He has sent our way, have we prayed?

And we who are called Christian counselors, do we pray with those who have come to us for emotional and spiritual healing? Again and again, toward the end of a session, I have had counselees say to me, "Would you please pray with me? I've talked with Dr. Christian Counselor several times, but when I ask him to pray with me, he refuses. He says that he only deals with my psychological problems, not the spiritual ones. I don't understand. I feel like I really need prayer."

No one is more sensitive to the misuse of prayer in the counseling process than I am. Ill-timed and ill-suited prayer can be damaging for some counselees. Some people's religious, yes, even Christian, concepts are so unbiblical, twisted, bizarre, and just plain sick that for me to pray with them could do more harm than good. It would give religious reinforcement to their unhealthy and neurotic brand of Christianity. In those instances, I spend a lot of time trying to help them clear up their distorted pictures of God and their caricatures of what He desires for them. So I am not talking about "quick fix" prayer or "zapping" which could be a coverup for our incompetence or failure to listen, or a substitute for adequately dealing with the deep roots of damaged emotions and painful memories which require healing.

However, *the answer to misuse is not disuse,* and as I expressed in chapter 1, I am deeply concerned by the lack of balance and scriptural integration in much that passes for Christian counseling today. There is a serious neglect of many of the *spiritual issues at the heart of counseling, including prayer.* For our goal is more than the healing of emotional problems. It is the wholeness and holiness which is essential to the process of sanctification. Our ultimate goal is not self-realization, self-confidence, or better self-esteem. These are wonderful serendipities of God's healing grace, which often cannot take place without the help of counseling and a support group. However, the true goal is a deeper self-surrender to our Lord, so that "in Christ" our true selves can be restored to the image of God, in whom and for whom we were created. And without prayer for and with our counselees, and without teaching them how to pray in healthy and constructive ways, this ultimate healing and wholeness cannot be achieved.

Jesus' miracles provide the clue to our use of prayer. Some people needed healing from disease; others needed recovery of sight for their eyes, or strength for a paralyzed limb; still others required release from the power of the evil one. And some had died; for them, healing or recovery was not enough. The dead had to be resurrected and restored to new life! If doing this required prayer by our Lord Himself, how much more it requires prayer by those temporary assistants of His who are called counselors!

● In addition to the fact that He prayed was the *pattern* of His prayer. Jesus did not begin by asking for anything. He began exactly the way He instructed us, His disciples, to begin our prayers, by reminding ourselves of our relationship to God, and the nature of His character (Matthew 6:9). And so Jesus' first word was "Father." Before any petition, He opened with worship, praise, and thanksgiving. I firmly believe that many of our troublesome "If onlys" would be cured *if only* we followed Jesus' example by beginning our prayers with thanksgiving and praise!

In his inspiring book, *In the Place of Immunity,* Francis Frangipane has used the story of Leah to emphasize this truth. Leah, Jacob's first wife, was unattractive, unwanted, and unloved by her husband. Jacob had worked hard for seven years for Rachel; but her wily father, Laban, tricked Jacob on the wedding night by putting her older sister, Leah, into the nuptial tent instead of Rachel. Although a week later Jacob also married Rachel, Laban forced him to work another seven years for her. So Jacob was married to two sisters: beautiful Rachel, whom he loved and desired, and unattractive Leah, whom he did not.

Then "the Lord saw that Leah was not loved" (Genesis 29:31). Francis Frangipane points out so beautifully that God's heart is drawn toward those who suffer from pain, loneliness, and heartache. So God gave her a son. Since this was Jacob's firstborn, Leah naturally said, "Surely my husband will love me now" (v. 32), but Jacob's heart was still closed toward her. This happened two more times, and again Leah thought, "Now at last my husband will become attached to me, because I have borne him three sons" (v. 34). Still, he did not love her. It all shows that it really is impossible to make someone love us. Sometimes, the harder we try the worse it gets. That was true for Leah, for now she felt jealous as well as rejected.

Then, during Leah's fourth pregnancy, a miracle of healing grace occurred in her heart. "She said, 'This time I will praise the Lord.' So she named him Judah" (v. 35). The name comes from the root word for *praise!* Frangipane reminds us that Jesus was born out of the tribe of Judah, and ultimately Leah was buried in a place of honor alongside such greats as Abraham, Sarah, Isaac, and Rebekah! (49:29-31) He comments with these significant words:

As we begin to praise Him in all things, we simultaneously put on the garments of salvation. We are actually being *saved* from that which would otherwise have destroyed us. Disappointments and heartaches cannot cling to us, for we are worshippers of God! And God causes all things to work for good to those who *love* Him.[1]

As long as Leah based her life on "If onlys' " — "If only I were beautiful like my sister," "If only my husband would love me" — her identity remained frozen as an unloved and unwanted victim. When she changed to praise and faith, she opened herself for God to give a new identity — the mother of the founder of the tribe through which the Messiah would come!

The same is true in our lives. The Scriptures constantly emphasize the importance of grounding our believing in thankfulness and praise. "In everything, by prayer and petition, with thanksgiving, present your requests to God" (Philippians 4:6). "Be joyful always; pray continually; give thanks in all circumstances, for this is God's will for you in Christ Jesus" (1 Thessalonians 5:16). This does not mean that we are forbidden to express painful feelings or should cover everything with a naive "Praise the Lord." It also does not mean that whatever takes place is thankworthy. Nor does it mean that whatever happens — a crippling accident, terminal cancer, the death of a child — is God's will, and therefore we are thankful *for* it. It is not thanking God for *things* which is His will. Rather, it is the *continuous giving of thanks* that is God's will for us. *It is God's will that we always praise Him in all circumstances.*

In *The Book of Common Prayer* we find The General Thanksgiving, which for centuries has drawn Christians into a spirit of praise. It begins with the Person of God and His goodness and love, His creation and preservation of us, His provision of redemption, and the hope of glory. And then the prayer beseeches God for a "due sense of all Thy mercies."

When you find yourself anxious and without a "due sense" of His mercies, enter into this prayer of praise.

THE GENERAL THANKSGIVING

Almighty God, Father of all mercies,
we thine unworthy servants
do give thee most humble and hearty thanks
for all thy goodness and loving-kindness
to us and to all men.
We bless thee for our creation, preservation,
and all the blessings of this life;
but above all for thine inestimable love
in the redemption of the world by our Lord Jesus Christ,
for the means of grace, and for the hope of glory.
And, we beseech thee,
give us that due sense of all thy mercies,
that our hearts may be unfeignedly thankful;
and that we show forth thy praise,
not only with our lips, but in our lives,
by giving up our selves to thy service,
and by walking before thee
in holiness and righteousness all our days;
through Jesus Christ our Lord,
to whom, with thee and the Holy Ghost,
be all honor and glory, world without end. Amen.[2]

If I Only Touch His Cloak, I Will Be Healed

The first three Gospels record the same story (Matthew 9:20-22; Mark 5:25-34; Luke 8:43-48), about a woman "who had been subject to bleeding for twelve years." Mark says, "She had suffered a great deal under the care of many doctors and had spent all she had, yet instead of getting better she grew worse" (5:26). Dr. Luke, like every good doctor I've known, does not speak disparagingly of his fellow physicians. His comment sounds like an official medical report, "No one could heal her."

It's important that we understand the background of this pathetic woman. By Jesus' day, the ancient Mosaic laws governing such an ailment (Leviticus 15:19-27) had become extremely rigorous and cruel. Therefore, this woman would have been excommunicated from both the temple and the synagogue, and excluded from all religious rites. Furthermore, by the same laws she would also have been divorced and cut off from any family life. Because anything she touched was considered contaminated by her uncleanness, she was ostracized as a social outcast. After spending all her money on doctors for twelve years, she no doubt lived in poverty. She was helpless and hopeless, truly a *victim* of medical ignorance, religious intolerance, and sexist prejudice.

But she "heard about Jesus." I wonder what? She could have heard plenty because He was literally "the talk of the town." According to Matthew's chronology, by then Jesus had healed Peter's mother-in-law, cleansed a leper, restored a paralytic, cast demons out of the possessed, and quieted a storm on the lake! She had heard much about this wonderful Man, enough for the information to change her desperation into determination. She said to herself, "If I only touch the edge of His cloak, I will be healed."

How different from saying, "If only I didn't have this awful disease," or "If only He would touch me, but of course He won't, because He's so pure He wouldn't risk defiling Himself." I can think of a dozen "If onlys" she might have said, and every one of them would have had a good reason behind it. But she didn't, for that would have been looking back with despair and blame and, as the saying goes, "She was sick and tired of being sick and tired!"

So she reversed it to "If I only touch . . . " That looks forward with desire and belief, not backward with complaint and blame. "If only" merely modifies the degree of the necessary action. She was saying, "From everything I've heard of this Jesus, I believe He has healing powers. And it won't take much on my part. *The only thing I need to do is to touch His cloak and I believe I will be healed!*" All three writers stress the size and pressure of the crowds surrounding Jesus. It must have been very difficult for her to get close to Him; and if the people had had any idea of her defiling affliction, they wouldn't have even allowed her to be in the crowd. It shows how firm and resolved her faith really was.

In our translations, the words *touch* and *cloak* are rather misleading. The Greek word for *touch* means "to grasp" and suggests the courage and the force of her action. And the word for *edge*, or *border* clearly means the cord or tassel on the fringe of a Rabbi's cloak, as prescribed by the law in Numbers 15:37-39, and mentioned in Matthew 23:5. This tassel can be seen today on an orthodox Jew's prayer shawl. In her desperation, this woman somehow pushed through every barrier and grasped that woven blue tassel at the bottom edge of Jesus' robe. And immediately she knew she had been healed! She had finished her mission, gotten what she came for; so now she tried to slip quietly away, unrecognized and unknown.

But Jesus was not finished with her. "Who touched [grasped] My clothes?" He asked, using the same word she had (Mark 5:30). He felt the "grasp" or tug on His cloak. The disciples protested in amazement because throngs of people were all pushing against Him, but Jesus knew this touch was different. His divine sensors told Him that someone had done more than just tug at His clothes. Someone had made the kind of contact that *pulled power from within Him.* Jesus knew the difference between a mere push or a pull and *a plug-in of faith!* The poor woman had been literally "caught in the act."

> Jesus kept looking around to see who had done it. Then the woman, knowing what had happened to her, came and fell at His feet and, trembling with fear, told Him the whole truth. He said to her, "Daughter, your faith has healed you. Go in peace and be freed from your suffering" (Mark 5:32-34).

The Blessings of Believing

What an incredible ending to a beautiful story. It contains some important truths for those of us who would turn from our futility to find freedom through faith.

● First, Jesus accepts us just where we are on the ladder of faith and lifts us up to a higher rung. We could criticize the woman's faith as being rather superstitious, or her action as a not very "spiritual" thing to do. There was certainly nothing mystical and magical about a tassel on Jesus' cloak. *He* was the Healer; *it* wasn't. But my years as a missionary among primitive peoples taught me that there are remarkable possibilities for faith at the heart of many religious actions and customs we might consider superstitious, weird, or strange. And Christian workers (counselors included) need to keep this in mind as we work among the sophisticated pagans of our land, "the new barbarians" as Charles Colson calls them, who are biblically illiterate and spiritually ignorant. The great Bible scholar G. Campbell Morgan reminds us, "It is well to remember that at the heart of superstition there may be faith. And where that is so, our Lord will ever answer the faith, and correct the superstition."[3] Jesus accepted her sincerity and honest confession as to why she had done what she did as a "grasp" of faith. In effect He said, "It was not My cloak but your faith in Me that healed you!"

How amazing is God's love in Christ for us! *How humble God is*, taking us any way He can get us, with never a, "Sorry, but you didn't do it the right way." He accepts us the way we are. All He wants us to do is to come to Him, fall at His feet in the kind of surrender which gives up all claim to our own sufficiency, tell Him the whole truth, and put our faith in Him.

I'm not sure who first began using this basic guideline for those in the kindergarten of faith. I learned it from Sam Shoemaker, the pastor who was the spiritual founder of Alcoholics Anonymous, and I have found it to be very effective with honest beginners. It is this simple proposition, *"Will you surrender as much of yourself as you understand to as much of Jesus Christ as you understand?"* I've found that if someone begins with an "If only" of surrendering, honest faith, then our Lord's power will lead the rest of the way.

● Second, Jesus healed her, cleansed her of her defilement, and gave her a whole new identity. According to tradition, when she touched Jesus He was supposed to become defiled. But exactly the opposite took place, because Christ's purity was always positive. His enemies criticized Him with, "He receives sinners." Worse yet, "He eats with them!" They thought that by such close contact with sinful people He would contract the contamination of their sins. They never realized it was the greatest compliment they could give Him. For rather than His being made unclean by their sins, they were made clean by His purity! This is why we can always affirm to everyone, however unclean they may be, that God loves them and will take them just the way they are. That's because He never leaves us the way we are. Joined to Him, we can never be or stay the same.

That's what happened to this woman. She came, ostracized, divorced, excommunicated, and considered by others to be defiled and defiling. All three writers agree about her *old identity* when she came to Jesus. And all three use the same word to describe the *brand new identity* Jesus gave her when He said, "DAUGHTER!"

Why have I made such a BIG DEAL of that? Because it is the *only time in the New Testament* that Jesus ever called anyone by that name. Wow! *From a nobody to a somebody to a daughter.* Jesus assured her she had been adopted into the family of God. Why only once and to this particular woman? Because Jesus considered her a *real victim* and knew she would face every imaginable difficulty. So He said, "Daughter, take heart, your faith has healed you" (Matthew 9:22). In other words, "Don't be afraid, for you are My daughter now. You belong to Me! Just as your faith has *healed* you, so your faith will also *hold* you in the difficult times ahead."

There's a very important word in this for some of us. For though our particular circumstances may be quite different from hers, we too know the loneliness, contamination, ostracism, and pain that she felt. Describing His mission, Christ said He had been sent "to heal the brokenhearted, to preach deliverance to the captives, and recovering of sight to the blind, to set at liberty them that are bruised" (Luke 4:18, KJV).

Some of us truly are victims, not only of physical disabilities but also of today's tragic emotional and spiritual ills . . . like the dys-grace of dysfunctional families, neglect and abandonment of children, betrayal and infidelity by spouses, physical violence and sexual abuse, divorce and hateful custody battles, and the heartbreak of children and grandchildren gone astray.

These and many more are the *bruises* which result in *bondage* to fear, to bitterness, to anxiety about relationships, to hatred of the opposite sex or revulsion or compulsion to sex in general, and to addictive behaviors. Some of us need all the help we can receive from social organizations, the church, counseling, and recovery groups. And in many instances, until there is a healing for the brokenness and deliverance from the power of these painful memories from the past, it is extremely difficult to exercise faith in God. However, after all is said and done, our ultimate wholeness will come only when we find release from the pain and captivity of our old identity, and then the joy and freedom of a new identity in Christ.

You may be thinking, "I'm glad Jesus personally said, 'Daughter' to that woman a long time ago. But what about us now?" Paul includes all of us when he tells us about the glory of "His grace, by which He made us accepted in the Beloved" (Ephesians 1:6, NKJV). "In the Beloved" . . . what does that strange phrase mean? Do you remember the Father's words at the baptism of Jesus? "This is My beloved Son, in whom I am well pleased" (Matthew 3:17, NKJV). Paul was reminding us, in a phrase he considered so important that he used it ninety times, that we are now "in Christ." That means we too are "in the Beloved." So we can listen *now* as God looks at each of us in Christ and gives us our *new identity*, "You are My beloved son, you are My beloved daughter, in whom I am well pleased."

Gaining a New Father

Let me illustrate this new identity by sharing a letter from Mary, who suffered a tragic loss when she was just a youngster.

> On Tuesday night your message spoke to me. Believe me, I could have been the president of the "If only" Society. I did not realize how much it had been harming me. I can never remember a time when I did not love the Lord, but lately, due to circumstances beyond my control, I could not sense His peace in my heart. I had previously tried many times to figure out which "If only" might have changed my life. I was sure when I lost my wonderful father at age twelve that all the rest

was caused by that loss. When you asked those who wanted to be set free to stand, I immediately rose to my feet and my wonderful husband did too. As you prayed I felt such a great peace come over me. I could hardly believe it. . . . When I went home I was afraid the joy of God's love and peace wouldn't last, but it did! Not every worry disappeared, but as they come toward me, instead of "If only" I say "If only I believe" and I "see the glory of God," and I am comforted!

The loss of a wonderful father at such a young age left not only a gaping hole in Mary's heart but also a painful "If only" which had held her in bondage for many years. But when she moved from blame to belief, she became the daughter of her Heavenly Father in an entirely new sense and felt embraced by His love and peace.

Yes, if we believe, miracles can happen even today. Heather Whitestone of Birmingham, Alabama was the victim of a childhood disease which left her almost totally deaf. She had no hearing in her right ear and only five percent in her left. But her mother had a strong faith in God and was determined Heather would grow up as normally as possible, and even learn how to talk. It took her six years just to learn to say her name! With a hearing aid in her left ear, she could barely hear vibrations, but grasping the rhythm she learned how to ballet dance. Many times she asked herself angrily, "Why me? Why did I have to be deaf?" But the anger was turned into energy to use every opportunity for creative action. When the other girls at school didn't want to be friends with her because of her handicap, her mother told her, "Don't feel sorry for yourself but for them. They've got a worse handicap than you have."

Then one incredible night in September 1994, the world watched and joyfully wept as beautiful, talented Heather danced so gracefully and conversed so winsomely that she was crowned Miss America 1995! It was the first time in its seventy-five-year history that a disabled person had won the contest. She said, "Anything is possible, if you work at it with God's help. In my family the word impossible didn't exist."[4] Yes, "If you will believe" you will see and hear, as victims become victors.

Sometimes this kind of miracle happens not only to people but to places. Do you remember when I told you how the Outcastes and Untouchables of India were forced to live in the *keri*, a segregated section of town? In 1896 the first Christian missionary went to Bidar, the town where we served as missionaries from 1946 to 1955. It took seven years of haggling and pleading to get the government to grant permission to purchase land so that the Methodist Mission could establish its work. As a kind of backhanded concession, the government finally allotted a large plot of land outside the walls of the city, and surrounded by several *keris*. Although it later proved to be an excellent location, at the time it was literally the city dump and considered worthless wasteland. Soon missionary housing, a school, a church, and a hospital were built on the site. Within a few years the mission hospital, staffed almost entirely by well-trained Indian Christian doctors and nurses, was overflowing with patients from every caste and religion who came from great distances to be treated. It became famous throughout the entire area and was the means of winning thousands to Christ. What had happened? *The city waste center had been transformed into the city health center!* Yes, long before Jesus said, "If you believe you will see the glory of God," Isaiah predicted that when the Messiah came, even the land would be transformed:

> The desert and the parched land will be glad;
> The wilderness will rejoice and blossom . . .
> They will see the glory of the Lord,
> The splendor of our God (35:1-2).

Lord, Just Say the Word and He Will Be Healed

Another great example of "If you believe" is the healing of the centurion's servant, found in Matthew 8:5-13 and Luke 7:1-10. Centurions were captains of the Roman army with 100 soldiers under their command. Seven of them are mentioned in the New Testament and every one is presented in a good light. But this man is really in a class by himself. Although he was a

Gentile, a foreigner, and a member of the hated army of occu-
pation, he was deeply loved by the Jewish people of the area.
Their elders pleaded with Jesus to grant his request, "because
he loves our nation and has built our synagogue" (Luke 7:5).
Just as remarkable was the fact that he showed such loving
concern for his servant, a man who would have been his bond-
slave. This was completely opposite from the typical Roman
attitude toward slaves, who were considered more like property
than persons. Obviously, this man had much higher ideals than
the nation he represented. And it was a person of such caliber
who entreated Jesus to heal his sick and suffering slave.

Jesus granted the request of the elders and went with them
toward the centurion's house. But He never got there, for the
centurion, having heard He was on the way, sent friends to
give Jesus this message:

> "Lord, don't trouble Yourself, for I do not deserve to have You
> come under my roof. That is why I did not even consider
> myself worthy to come to You. But say the word, and my
> servant will be healed. For I myself am a man under authority,
> with soldiers under me. I tell this one, 'Go,' and he goes; and
> that one, 'Come,' and he comes. I say to my servant, 'Do this,'
> and he does it."
>
> When Jesus heard this, He was amazed at him, and turning
> to the crowd following Him, He said, "I tell you, I have not
> found such great faith even in Israel." Then the men who had
> been sent returned to the house and found the servant well
> (Luke 7:6-10).

What a remarkable contrast to one of the negative "If onlys"
we looked at in chapter 7, the kind that excuse sins and failures
by saying, "If only God would do something spectacular!" The
centurion illustrated the principle we discussed then, for in his
moral quality, he was walking in the light he *had* received, living
by that which he *did* understand, and not waiting for some dra-
matic new disclosure. His heart, therefore, was open and prepared
to believe when the Light of the World shone his way. And
believe he did, with an incredible "If" of faith. "Lord," he said,
"You don't need to come to my house; I'm not worthy of that. If
You only say the word, I know he will be healed!"

The reasoning behind his great faith is profound. Don't miss both sides of his rationale about authority, for it is the basis of his faith — and ours as well. Remember, no true Roman was to recognize any authority except, "Caesar is Lord." But he, in effect, said to Jesus, *"Lord, You are the ultimate authority. I understand who You are and the power and authority You have.* Because I myself am *under* authority, I have to obey a *higher* authority. But I also have soldiers under my authority who have to obey my orders." The way he used "I myself" — translated in all the older versions as "I also" — is deeply significant. He understood that Christ was *in authority* because He was *under authority. Christ had power because He had been given it by a higher power.* He recognized and declared that Christ was *in* authority so that everything would obey Him, because Christ was *under* the One who had all authority and the power to enforce it!

What amazing insight into the One who constantly said that He had no power or authority in Himself, but that it had all been given to Him by the Father. And what amazing foresight toward the day Jesus would say, "All authority in heaven and on earth has been given to Me." This centurion, this Gentile foreigner in Israel, put the deepest and most difficult theological truth into simple military language that everyone could understand!

Now we know why Jesus was astonished, and said to the crowd, "I tell you, I have not found such great faith even in Israel!" There are many places in the Gospels where we are told that people "marveled" at something Jesus said or did. But only twice does it say that Jesus "marveled" at anything. In this incident He "marveled at his faith." In the synagogue at Nazareth, "He marveled at their unbelief" (Mark 6:6). In both instances, the issue of obedience or disobedience was crucial. Perhaps we should ask ourselves, "Which of these characteristics does He see in us to cause Him to marvel?"

Believing and Obeying

All through Scripture, believing and obeying are inseparably linked together, both as cause and consequence. In Hebrews 11 almost every instance of great faith is illustrated by obedient action, often in the most everyday, practical matters. By faith *Noah* built an ark. By faith *Abraham* started on a journey without knowing the destination. By faith *Sarah and Abraham* had a baby. By faith *Moses' parents* hid a baby. By faith *Joshua* marched around some walls. And the list goes on. Did they have no fears, no doubts, no questions? Read their stories and you'll get a quick answer to that! But "by faith" they acted and they risked. They obeyed and believed, believed and obeyed.

Years ago, when I was just starting to counsel, a suggestion from Dietrich Bonhoeffer helped me greatly. If I were to summarize it in one sentence it would be this, "Sometimes we have to believe in order to obey, and at other times we have to obey in order to believe." Bonhoeffer says we must keep both sides of this truth in balance. If we do not, we will be guilty of "cheap grace" on the one side or "salvation by works" on the other, either of which is just "another word for damnation."[5]

The evening service was over and it was late. All the seekers except Larry had left the altar of the church, and members of the prayer team were getting weary. Larry had been given many Bible verses and some well-meaning but conflicting advice, "Hold on," "Let go," "Just believe," and a few other pious pushes. But Larry kept insisting, "I'm sorry, I really want to, but I just don't seem able to believe." I stood back, listening and waiting. Finally, when he started to leave, I asked if I could walk with him back to the men's dorm on campus. He reluctantly but respectfully agreed. As we walked along, I told him as tenderly and toughly as I could that I had heard some things lately. . . . Something about the fact that a few guys had broken into the science building and gotten a copy of the quarterly exam. And that I'd heard his name mentioned among them. Larry stopped, looked at me incredulously, and then, with a pained expression, admitted it was true. I told him that maybe this helped us understand why he "just couldn't believe."

I made him a proposition. I offered to run interference for him if he'd carry the ball for the touchdown. I would go and see the science professor, and pave the way for him to come and make things right. We had a brief prayer together and I left it with him. Two days later he phoned and agreed to the plan. The science professor accepted his confession and gave him an F on that exam. But then he went the extra mile. He offered to help him study for the next exams, so he might possibly pull up his grades and pass the course. Larry barely made it, but he did pass the course. All this resulted in his conversion. He is now a committed Christian businessman, and for years has been active as a leader in his church and community. He had to obey in order to believe, just as others have to believe in order to obey.

All this reminds me of a friend who was preaching in a small, rural church where there was no sound system. He noticed a man with his hand cupped behind his ear. Finally he stopped, increased his volume a little, and said to the man, "Excuse me, Sir, do you want me to speak a little louder?"

"Oh, no," the man replied at once, "I'm already *hearing* a lot more than I'm *doing!*"

Just as hearing and doing belong together, so do believing and obeying. The old song is right, "Trust and Obey, for there's no other way . . ."

A Small and Imperfect Faith

"Bigger is better," we often say, which infers that biggest is best. What is the biggest living thing in all the world? An elephant, a whale, a giant tree in a California forest? No, nothing as beautiful or awesome as those. The biggest living creature is a humongous fungus, a massive underground blob growing in the woods just over, or rather under, the Wisconsin-Michigan border. It feeds off rotting organic matter and tree roots and has been doing so for the last 1,500 years. The thing already covers a whopping twenty-seven acres, and weighs around 1,000 tons. And it is still growing. This mass of subterranean cytoplasm has the amusing scientific name of *Armillaria bulbosa*. Ultimately it will produce a plague of mushrooms which will pop up out of the ground and spread rapidly.

But not to worry. At its present rate of creep, it will not reach the city of Milwaukee for another 1.6 million years![6]

Jesus didn't believe that biggest is best. And for that matter, neither do scientists. Most important research and discovery today seems to be in the direction of the microscopically small, like DNA, computer microchips, or tiny, life-giving implants.

Just how big and perfect does our faith need to be? Jesus gave us the answer in an important "If" of faith. When the disciples asked Him why they were unable to perform a miracle of deliverance, He told them, "Because you have so little faith. I tell you the truth, if you have faith as small as a mustard seed, you can say to this mountain, 'Move from here to there' and it will move. Nothing will be impossible for you" (Matthew 17:20-21). Once again Jesus stressed the power of the small by comparing the kingdom of God to a mustard seed, "Though it is the smallest of all your seeds, yet when it grows, it is the largest of garden plants" (Matthew 13:32).

Perhaps you are thinking, "I understand that we don't have a large amount of faith, but surely the small amount we do have must be a pure faith, without any mixture of doubts, questionings, or unbelief." Because many people do think this, I believe we need to combine the "If" of "only as small as a mustard seed" with another "if you believe" passage.

It's that touching story of the father who brought his son to Jesus for healing and release from an evil spirit (Mark 9:14-29). At first the father was not sure that Jesus had the power to accomplish it. "If You can do anything, take pity on us and help us."

" 'If You can'?" said Jesus, almost scoldingly. "Everything is possible for him who believes."

And immediately the boy's father exclaimed, "I do believe; help me overcome my unbelief!"

Now we all know how the story ended. When Jesus heard that, He said to the man, "Well, it's quite obvious that you do not have a pure enough faith to really believe that I can do it." And Jesus turned to Peter and asked him if they would be coming near this place when they returned from their evangelistic tour. Peter looked in his little black datebook, which all good preachers carry, and said, "Yes, Lord, it just happens that three weeks from now we will be coming quite nearby." So Jesus said to the father, "Why don't you take your boy and return home, and work on your faith. See if you can't get rid of all those doubts and build up a sufficient faith. Then come back and bring your son with you, and I'll see what I can do for him. But do try harder to believe."

No! No! No! Aren't you glad that Jesus isn't like that? What really did happen? The moment Jesus saw the father's deep desire and sincere struggle to believe, and heard his desperate cry for help, Jesus honored his small and imperfect faith and healed his son. It's the difference between *avis* which is English for "I'll try harder," and *charis* which is Greek for "grace and gift," and prays, "Lord, help me overcome my unbelief by graciously giving me the gift of faith." It's the difference between "If only" you will try harder to trust, and "If you only" realize that in your own strength you are not even able to trust, unless God grants you the grace of believing.

A Mustard Seed Growing in a Strange Place

A British missionary serving as a nurse in an Anglican Hospital tells of this incredible experience.[7] The hospital is located in Peshawar, on the northwest border of Pakistan, a rugged, mountainous region where fierce tribesmen live. They are much like the guerilla fighters of Afghanistan who recently defeated the Russians. They are tall, strong, fearless warriors, and fanatically Muslim in their religion.

Into the mission hospital one day stumbled Dick, an unshaven, dirty, wandering American hippie. Not only was he addicted to drugs, which are dirt-cheap in that area, but he had venereal disease and hepatitis. Dick stayed several weeks until he was better, but when he left, he wandered amid the hills hoping to get high on drugs. One day, an older tribesman named Ahmed found Dick unconscious on the path near his village. His Muslim religion dictated that he show compassion on a stranger and foreigner. So he picked him up and carried him to his own home, where he and his family cared for him. Years before Ahmed had fought in the British army, so he knew enough English to communicate with Dick. He understood about his drug problem and, realizing he could not live without it, even supplied him with drugs. After many weeks Dick was almost well, but still totally enslaved to drugs.

One day Ahmed, who had become genuinely fond of his young American friend, talked to him about giving up his drugs. Dick assured him he had tried many times but found it utterly impossible. Finally Ahmed urged him to pray to Jesus to deliver him from his terrible habit. Faint memories of a childhood Sunday School stirred deep inside Dick. In his complete helplessness and desperation, he cried out, "Jesus, help me, help me to believe in You. Jesus, help me." And wonder of wonders, the Lord answered his prayers and delivered Dick from his habit!

Some weeks later, shaven, clean, looking and acting completely different, Dick came back to the hospital and told the nurse what had happened. She couldn't believe it. It was impossible, for she knew that Ahmed was a devout Muslim. She waited until Ahmed brought a grandson to the hospital for treatment to ask him about Dick's unbelievable story. He assured her that every detail was true.

"But how could it be, Ahmed? Are you a Christian?" she asked.

"Oh, no, Madam. Allah is my God and Mohammed is his prophet."

"But Ahmed, then why did you tell him to pray to Jesus?"

He was quiet for a moment. "Oh, Madam," he replied, "for ordinary people, religious people like us, it's all right. But we know in such cases, like Dick, when there is no hope, when the power of Sythan (Satan) has full hold on the person, then there is only one name to pray to. Only the prophet Jesus can save from Sythan's power!"

"If you will only believe." Yes, even if a devout Muslim, on a rugged mountainside in a distant and hostile land, plants a tiny mustard seed of faith in the heart of a lost and enslaved American hippie, a mountain will move, and we "will see the glory of God."

---

*"Jesus said to them,
'Take off the grave clothes
and let him go.' "*

9

Group Grace

Martha and Mary stood spellbound at the open tomb. As Jesus had been praying, their faith was growing. They were beginning to believe. He had just finished His prayer when He called in a loud voice, "Lazarus, come out!" Along with everyone else, their eyes strained to pierce the shadows at the entrance of the tomb. Then they heard a strange scraping sound, as if somebody was dragging his feet on the ground. And suddenly the crowd cried out with amazement as "the dead man came out, his hands and feet wrapped with strips of linen, and a cloth around his face" (John 11:44). Jesus had told them that they would see the glory of God, and now they certainly did. The terrible ordeal of the last four days, an ordeal which seemed to them like four years, was finally over!

Or was it? Jesus turned to speak. No doubt He had a final word of welcome and encouragement for Lazarus. Instead, He turned until He no longer faced the tomb and the resurrected Lazarus, but was looking straight at the two sisters and their friends. Then He said to them, "Take off the grave clothes and let him go."

The message was plain: Jesus had done what only *He* could do, by the power of *God's grace*. Now they must do what only *they* could do, by the power of *group grace*. Jesus affirmed the divine-human division of labor, even in God's miracle of healing and restoring people to new life. He made clear that the human part remained to be done. Jesus didn't do it and He didn't ask Lazarus to do it. He asked *them* to do it, "Unbind him and let him go" (RSV). This was something they could do only by working together. Life is filled with tasks like that.

An amazing incident took place in Detroit in the summer of 1936. In order to accommodate the growing downtown traffic problems, the city government decided to widen Woodward Avenue, the city's main traffic artery. There was only one major problem: On Woodward Avenue in the heart of the city stood Central Methodist Church, representing the oldest Protestant Society in the State of Michigan. Since 1860 the great spire of that church had pointed people toward God and was a familiar landmark of Detroit. There was no other alternative, so finally the order was given for the avenue to be widened. They would tear down the tower and spire, and take twenty-four feet from that side of the building.

The church fathers knew they had to comply, but was there a way out? The finest engineers were called in, but all they did was shake their heads and knit their brows. At last it was decided that they would save the tower and the spire at all costs. To do this they would cut off a portion of the church and then relocate the spire twenty-four feet to the east and six feet to the south!

Now the most amazing thing of all was the fact that Detroit, with all its engineering genius, had no single machine strong enough and delicate enough to move that spire. After all, it was 182 feet high and weighed 2,000 tons! In Detroit they had moved entire banks, hotels, and even apartment houses, but something as tall and fragile as that spire baffled them.

Finally, after Lloyds of London agreed to insure the move, a clever engineer came up with the solution. They would move the spire tower by putting seven great roller-jacks underneath it. Then they would select seven strong men who would learn to turn those jacks by hand in rhythmic unison. So they built the scaffolding and the huge jacks, and the men practiced together for days. The night before it was to be done, the engineer in charge was flooded by thousands of phone calls from Detroiters of every race and creed. They had grown to love that old spire so much that they wanted to make sure he knew what he was doing. Finally, he left his home and slept in the park with his face turned all night toward that lonely tower — praying!

Before the city was awake they began the job. A trained leader stood before the seven men and directed them just as if he were leading an orchestra. The men carefully turned all the jacks together in precise unison; the spire moved four inches. The engineer in the park trembled as he watched. It was so smoothly done that the pigeons in the belfry never even fluttered their wings! So they moved it a few more inches. Then, every morning for the next two weeks, the seven men turned their jacks. And they successfully moved that spire twenty-four feet east and six feet south! A group of people working together did what no one person — or machine — could do.

When Lazarus was restored to life, he was barely able to come out of the tomb. After his death the sisters had carefully prepared him for burial by sprinkling spices over his body and wrapping it in strips of linen cloth. The trunk of his body was wrapped in one section, then each leg and foot, arm and hand bandaged separately, and finally his face and head in yet another cloth. Bound up this way he was able only with great difficulty to stumble out of the grave.

Jesus' Word to Those Who Need to Be Unbound

Lazarus was helpless to take off the strong strips of cloth in which he had been so tightly wrapped. He desperately needed to be unwound and unbound, loosened and set free. Jesus Himself recognized that the task was not complete. Lazarus still had to be fully released from every vestige of the grave. This is a striking picture of a sobering fact. Most of us will not experience the healing and restoration we need unless we allow others to unbind us from the grave clothes of our past.

There is a simple psychological/spiritual principle in all this: Most of our barriers to grace and belief are the result of unhealthy, destructive, or sinful relationships in the past. These bruise, bind, and imprison us in ways of death, not life. And so we turn to flight or fight, freeze or fondling, or we try to fool ourselves and others, and so develop wrong ways of dealing with life and relating to people. These patterns become ways of quiet desperation, surviving, or merely existing in a kind of a living death. They are the old, smelly, rotten models from the past which keep us bound up and tied down. The only way these grave clothes will be removed is through experiencing healthy, constructive personal relationships in the present. These take place in an atmosphere of intimacy and trust. And, as Gordon MacDonald puts it so well,

> Intimacy is not going to happen in the congregation, when people look at the back of one another's heads. . . . The mega church . . . will not survive over a long period of time without incorporating healthy small groups. People cannot be nourished in large meetings alone. Anyone who is going to grow in the faith is going to need some type of small group.[1]

The key to the small group is, of course, an atmosphere of openness to one another as a means of developing deeper openness to God.

More Open Than Usual

Norman Grubb, noted Keswick Conference speaker of an earlier generation, often compared the Christian life to a person inside a house, enclosed by four walls which hold up the roof. The walls are the sins which separate us from other people, and keep us from loving our neighbors as we should, sins such as lust, selfishness, resentment, unforgiveness, dishonesty, pride, and spiritual pretense. The roof represents our disobedience and unbelief which separate us from God. In our initial salvation experience, Grubb would say, the Holy Spirit blows a hole in the roof of the house. This opens the way for relationship with God, and we begin to have communion and fellowship with Him. Then, through reading the Word, praying, and other spiritual disciplines, we constantly try to enlarge that opening in the roof, so that we can grow in grace and in our fellowship with God. But after a while we make an important discovery: if we will knock down the walls which separate us from one another, then *the roof will come down all by itself!* He stressed that although such an action is usually costly, it is highly rewarding. For by opening ourselves to one another, we always open ourselves to God in new and greater ways.

During the terrible German air raids on London during World War II, most of the population sought shelter in the deep underground subway stations. After the air raids were over and the all-clear sirens sounded, thousands of people would come streaming up into the streets, causing considerable confusion. During those times, a merchant who operated a small grocery store discovered that he was losing business because people in his neighborhood didn't know whether he had returned safely and reopened his store. So he painted a sign with large letters and hung it over the front entrance. The sign read, OPEN AS USUAL. It proved to be helpful and his business picked up immediately. Then one day a bomb fell close by and blew away part of the front of his store. Because of the scarcity of materials, it took some time to repair the damage. Although he did the best he could with what he had, it still looked a bit shabby because some gaps and holes remained visible. So he decided to add something to the sign. When the customers returned to his store, the sign read, MORE OPEN THAN USUAL!

The New Testament contains many appeals for us to be "more open than usual," and emphasizes the importance of honest transparency with one another. James makes group grace necessary to full healing and restoration. "Therefore confess your sins to each other and pray for each other so that you may be healed" (5:16).

From its earliest beginnings the church was based on group grace. "Now the company of those who believed were of one heart and soul, and no one said that any of the things he possessed was his own, but they had everything in common" (Acts 4:31, RSV). We might assume this refers only to their possessions, but I remind you that the reason they gave *things* to each other is that they first gave *themselves* to one another. "Everything" included the truth about themselves and pretenses about their own goodness. There were very few "good Christians" in that company. Peter never let himself and his hearers forget about his betrayal of Jesus, and James wrote about gossip, snobbery, and other sins, as if he knew them "from the inside." Nobody ever dreamed they could go it alone or do it by themselves.

What a tragedy that this openness got lost in the third century with the practice of private confession which finally resulted in the "sealing of the confessional." As every counselor knows, valuable as private confession is, it often fails to deal with the core of many of our problems—*our failure to break through pride and pretense and to reveal to God and others our true selves.*

The power of small-group grace was rediscovered on a large scale during the great evangelical revival in Britain under the Wesleys. Church historians give full credit to the Spirit-anointed preaching of John Wesley and the inspiring hymns of Charles Wesley for generating the revival. But all agree it was the incredible power of those small groups, the "societies" and "bands" with their weekly meetings, which brought about the *lasting transformation* of individuals and the nation. These small groups, never more than twelve seekers and beginners, many of whom had literally been scooped out of the scum of society, met weekly to study Scripture, share their sins and victories, and pray together. How tragic that they were abandoned until secular recovery groups discovered their tremendous power to change people. So the roots of AA, and similar organizations, can be traced back to definite Christian principles, back through the Episcopalian clergyman Sam Shoemaker to the Oxford movement and to the early Methodist Societies.

Support, Accountability, and Prayer

Every period of history seems to be characterized by certain kinds of sins and problems. Because we are a culture of great affluence, we are highly susceptible to addictions related to our "affluenza," like chemical highs, drugs, alcohol, homosexuality, promiscuity, various kinds of sexual compulsions including pornography, gambling, spending, gluttony, eating disorders, and an amazing variety of sick dependencies. Many of us are modern Lazaruses. Although we have experienced the miracle of new life in Christ, we are still bound by the grave clothes of these sins, whether committed against us or by us or both.

A lifetime of pastoral counseling has taught me that the badly bound among us will never be truly healed, restored, and set free without the basic ingredients of group grace. All the small groups in which I have been involved have, in one form or another, contained three essential elements. First, loving acceptance and personal support. Second, confrontation and accountability. Third, individual and united prayer. Again and again a vital part of my personal counseling ministry was to get people not only into the body life of the church at large, but also into some kind of smaller group, "the church within the church."

It has been wonderful to witness and experience the process at work, as members give loving acceptance without criticism or judgment when others openly share their sins, temptations, and failures. For example, in a group dealing with sexual addictions, everyone was asked to write out their complete sexual history. Sometimes the erotic autobiography was a "shocker," but nobody reacted to the rotten, stinking grave clothes. "We understand" was their chief comment. I was often reminded of Paul's description of how he began his work among the Thessalonians, "Our attitude among you was one of tenderness, rather like that of a nurse caring for her babies. Because we loved you" (1 Thessalonians 2:8, PH).

Tender Toughness

But don't confuse this with some kind of general discussion group with its monotonous, never-ending, "How do you feel?" question. Paul quickly adds that he was also "like a father with his children. We exhorted each one of you, encouraged you, and charged you to lead a life worthy of God" (2:11, RSV). This aspect was so evident in the small groups, for here were people who loved and cared for one another by watching over each other. I often heard, "If I miss church nobody seems to notice. But if I miss the group, I can expect a phone call within hours!" Their care was further shown by confronting and holding each other accountable, for they knew all the excuses and had used them too many times themselves. All the "If onlys" of blaming someone else — "I saw Dad's porno magazines when I was just a kid," or "I'm not that bad, I just slip a little sometimes" — they had heard them all and knew that all the rationalizations came from the one who is "the father of lies." So they loved and labored with each other, sometimes as patient as a mother, or as tough as a boxer, sometimes giving deep insights from helpful psychological studies and at other times sharing a Scripture which had helped them.

And always they prayed for one another, individually, over the phone, or together as a group in "agreed" prayer. Constantly they plugged into the most high-voltage "If" of faith Jesus ever promised:

> I tell you the truth, whatever you bind on earth will be bound in heaven, and whatever you loose on earth will be loosed in heaven.
> Again, I tell you that if two of you on earth agree about anything you ask for, it will be done for you by My Father in heaven. For where two or three come together in My name, there am I with them (Matthew 18:18-20).

They literally unwound the grave clothes and "loosed" what had been bound!

At times I have used an extreme illustration for dealing with some of the most tenacious problems, the kinds which cause truly honest people to say, "I'm all tied up," or "I'm hung up," or "I just can't seem to cut loose from him or her or it!" Some folks ask, "How long do these people have to stay in a support or recovery group? Do they need it permanently?" My own experience convinces me that certain kinds of addictions, especially those which involve sexual deviations or chemical and substance dependencies, are often lengthy, sometimes even lifelong. For other people, however, it would be a mistake to stay in a special group for too long. If they do, the cure can become part of the problem as these people get stuck in the past. Or, the group itself becomes the object of their focus and energy. A group should never take the place of Christ and the body life of His church.

However, there are many other opportunities for tapping into the transforming power of group grace, such as Bible study groups, Christian recovery groups, groups on divorce recovery, book discussion groups using accompanying workbooks or leader's guides, small Sunday School classes, groups for singles and married couples, parenting classes, and a host of others.

While we ministered to seminary students, my wife, Helen, started a Bible study, prayer, and share group for the "cabin-fevered wives of seminarians." These were the wives with children who chose not to work outside the home. They often faced financial problems, but most of all, sheer loneliness and hard work. Their husbands were away at school most of the day and studying in the library until late at night. They were motivated by exciting new ideas and fellowship with other students, while the wives were "emotionally dying on the vine." Part of our tithe provided childcare when the mothers came to the parsonage every Wednesday morning. This went on for fifteen years until our house could no longer accommodate the numbers. Many hurts and tears were shared, prayers answered, lives changed, and deep canyons of need filled with love and joy. The group has continued long after our retirement, is now held in the church, and is largely self-perpetuating. The best part is that it has multiplied like a spiritual amoeba, for many of those pastors' wives have started similar small groups wherever they have gone.

Free at Last

Years ago at a conference I witnessed the unbinding power of group grace. Jack and Lucille and their two children had traveled quite a distance to attend—they were getting "near the bottom of their hope barrel." I counseled with Lucille just once and, with her permission, had prayed that God would reveal her true need. She faithfully took part in all the services and the small-group sessions. The meeting was to close with a general time of witnessing to what God had done for us. After several had shared, Lucille arose, was silent until she could get better control of her tears, and then said to the group:

> I don't understand what's wrong with me. All week I've run from all of you. Each message made me more miserable, and each group more uncomfortable. Yet all of you have been wonderful to me. You've tried to love me, but I just wouldn't let you. I've watched love overflow for me out of my husband all these years, but it's only made me all the angrier. My little girl has tried to love me, but I've slapped her around. This week I've finally admitted to myself that what I've really wanted all my life was to be loved and to love. But I've never been able to do it, because I've never been able to accept God's love. I've resented God and I haven't even been grateful for a wonderful husband and two wonderful kids. And this week I've seen it through all of you, and especially through my little girl. I've seen all of you love her, and the way she's responded to your love, and it's been so amazing. And it's made me so empty.

By now her voice had risen until she was almost screaming. She began to talk half to us and half to God. She turned her face upward and cried out, "O God, please forgive me. I've been so proud, so hard, and so unloving." Now she was praying loudly and weeping openly.

A well-meaning minister interrupted her, saying, "Let's all sing a song together." Isn't it amazing how uncomfortable we preachers get when God's Spirit is disturbing someone and we can't fix it! I was the leader in charge, and quick as a flash I started to refute his suggestion. But I didn't need to, for Lucille immediately said, "No, No, let me go on. I'm just starting, and I want to finish." All of a sudden she let out a loud cry of joy. "Oh, thank You, God. I'm free! I'm free! It's gone. I feel free for the first time in my life. Thank You, God!"

Meanwhile, her little girl who was in the nearby childcare

room had heard her mother crying out. She came running into the room and said, "O Mama, Mama, what's wrong?" and with a leap jumped up and started hugging her mother around the neck. By now her husband, Jack, was also weeping, and Lucille grabbed him and all three began hugging each other. It was an electrifying moment. About twenty African-Americans were part of the group and they started singing and praising God. I then asked some volunteers to join me, and as the family knelt, we laid hands on them and prayed for their total healing. Sounds like a Pentecostal tent meeting, doesn't it? But it happened at a very conservative Mennonite college! And Jack and Lucille ended up in the Episcopal ministry. Lucille had been a Christian and in the church for many years, but was finally untied and set free only by the power of group grace.

On *Eye to Eye*, October 28, 1993, Connie Chung interviewed a man named Bloodsworth. For nine years he had been on death row in the Maryland State Penitentiary, charged with rape and murder. Finally a DNA test proved him innocent. When they called him with the news, he dropped the phone and went running down the corridor shouting in front of each cell, "I'm free, I'm free!" The final scene of the story showed him outside the prison in his car. Both the front and back license plates read, "FREE!"

Jesus' Word to Those Who Do the Unbinding

I want now to talk about the meaning of the small group for those of us who are called to do the unbinding. How often, after Jesus has done great miracles in people's lives, miracles so incredible they could only be compared to a resurrection from the dead, we fail to do what He has asked us to. With our old thoughts and attitudes toward the people who need release, we continue to keep them wrapped up in the grave clothes of their former lives. How often we hold to our negative, skeptical, pre-resurrection points of view which make it difficult, if not impossible, for them to break out of the old ways in which they have been wrapped up. Here's a place where the two "Ifs" belong together.

If we believe, we will see the *glory* and if only we were as quick to obey Jesus in unwrapping those within our care as Martha and Mary were in unbinding Lazarus, we'd see even *greater glory!*

Consider some of the people and areas in our lives where Jesus would say to us, "Unbind them and let them go." Perhaps He would have us begin where Martha and Mary did, *in our homes* with our nearest and dearest. Take, for example, our *spouses.* We know them better than anyone else, or at least we think we do. We understand their nature and their characteristics, their ways of doing and saying and responding. We know all their *idiosyncrasies.*

Thinking of all mine, Helen says that word comes from three Old English words, *idiot, sin,* and *crazy!* Actually, the word is made up of three Greek words, *person, with,* and *mixture,* a person of mixed temperament! And we who live closest to them know all the various characteristics in their mixture. Tragically, we often think they cannot change, and say to ourselves that they've been in that "grave" too many years. We wrap our partners around and around until they can never stir beyond our old attitudes and expectations of them. Yet maybe it's not a grave, but just a rut. There's a big difference, because a rut is still open at both ends! Perhaps if we unbind them and let them go, they will be able to walk out of the rut and change.

I remember a couple who gave their testimonies at a Lay Witness Mission in our church. She said, "For years I just couldn't stand my husband and many of his strange ways. I especially resented his opposition to my religion and church life. I used to pray, 'Lord, You *love* him, and I'll *change* him.' Then one day, while I was muttering that prayer under my breath, I seemed to hear God saying to me, 'Millie, you've got it all wrong. You love him and let Me change him.' " She added that by God's grace that's what she did, and within two years he was converted and had joined the church. Now they go around giving their combined witness for Christ.

The same can be said about our children. As their parents

we think we know them best. After all, we've loved and cared for them since before they were born. We've had to be hands and feet and eyes and minds for them. We've been pediatricians and pharmacists, teachers and trainers, cooks and coaches for them. We've nursed them through sickness and nurtured them through health. We've sacrificed for them, prayed for them, loved them, and sometimes been so mad at them we wanted to kill them. I never really understood child abuse until my kids went through the terrible twos! We know them or think we do, until they become teenagers or young adults, and one day the neighbor or the youth minister or the school principal or the police call us up.

And then we realize that, like it or not, we have to "loose them, and let them go." No, not from the wrappings of the grave, but from the "swaddling clothes" of the cradle, or the kiddie clothes of childhood, or whatever we have had them wrapped in. They are no longer just ours, and it is wrong for us to try to keep them bound and controlled just to satisfy our own need for them. I can tell you, as a missionary and pastor, what a great temptation it has been to keep our kids bound tightly, and sacrifice them to the necessity of maintaining a good reputation as parents.

I've heard a sentence similar to this from scores of kids who came out of "good Christian homes," or who were PKs or MKs. "I know it probably wasn't true, but as I was growing up my folks acted as if they cared much more about how I affected their reputation than they did for me as a person."

Jesus would say to some of us, "Unbind them, let them go, let them grow. I know it's risky, because they may not walk exactly as you had planned for them. But untie them, and let them make their own decisions and live with the results. Stand by them, but don't stand in their way. And, above all, believe in them and tell them that you do. Have faith in them, even when they've lost faith in themselves! You have given them life, and I will give them new life. Relinquish them into My hands and keep your hand on them only in prayer. They belong not only to you, but also to Me.

Love knows when to hang on, and love knows when to let go. Loose them and let them go, for I love them even more than you do!"

The Irregular People in Our Lives

I used to have an antique roll-top desk. I loved it, with all its little compartments, drawers, and pigeonholes for my office supplies. At least it enabled me to keep my mess organized. Remembering it leads to my confession. As I look back at my early years as a new Christian, I see where I committed a grave sin. In my zeal to be all-out for Christ I pigeonholed people, classifying them spiritually so that they fit into neat categories. There were the "Saved," the "Spirit-filled," the "Worldly," the "Shallow," and so on *ad nauseam*. With regard to these irregular people, those who were different from me, I failed to hear Jesus' "Unbind them." I made pigeonhole graves which entombed people. But the truth was that the pigeonholes entombed me, and I cheated myself out of fellowship and enrichment with a lot of wonderful Christians.

Even worse than that, I kept some unreached people wrapped in the grave clothes of their sins, instead of allowing the life-giving power of Christ to work in their lives. I had preconceived pictures of what they should be and would be "If only" they did or didn't do this or that. Instead of wrapping them about with my love and God's love, I kept them bandaged in some ready-made designs of my own ideas of righteousness.

Eugenia Price, well-known Christian speaker and author, tells in *The Burden Is Light* of the part her friend Ellen Riley played in her conversion and subsequent growth in grace. With deepest appreciation she recounts how Ellen stuck by her after her first Christian beginnings, in spite of the fact that she kept up her incessant chain-smoking, and slipped into profanity. Even when she had a bad setback and denied everything for a brief period, Ellen would not tie her back into the grave clothes of her old life. She kept loving and loosening and leading her, sometimes at considerable risk to her own spiritual reputation. Listen to what Eugenia says about Ellen in another one of her books, "I testify from my own experience that if the one who led me to Christ had in any way, by the merest shadow of inference, chanced to condemn me during those first tense days as the Holy Spirit worked in my heart, I would not be writing these lines now."[2]

How grateful I am for the way God forced me to push back my horizons by simply dumping me into so many different situations, with so many different kinds of people with whom He was obviously working in so many different ways. Slowly but surely, my narrow and limited view of God and His methods became enlarged. Best of all, as He taught me how to take off the wrappings in which I had bound up others so tightly, He was able to loosen me from my own grave clothes and set me free to allow Him to work as He desired. How much my life has been enriched by discovering the incredible ways God uses to get through to people!

Jesus is speaking His Word of "unbinding" to some of us who are in His service. He is telling us to maintain a hopeful, redemptive attitude toward everyone, to stop canonizing their deficiencies and setting their sins and faults in concrete. He is reminding us that a lot of people are no better than they are because we have never believed they could be better. They have not changed because we did not have faith that they could be changed. We have not only kept them bound, but we have also bound the hands of God who wanted to free them. Love "believes all things," and faith "believes all things are possible with God."

After many weeks of counseling a young man, it was obvious that he had reached a point of decision. The risk of giving up all his old "If onlys" really frightened him. He said he was "trying hard to believe" that he could be changed, but wasn't making much progress in that direction. As he was about to leave, I said almost offhandedly, "Don't worry, Tom, I've got enough faith for both of us." It didn't seem to register, for he made no reply and I didn't observe a flicker of hope in his expression. That afternoon he was to meet with a bunch of guys in a small prayer group. He felt so discouraged that he almost didn't go, but at the last minute decided to attend. He shared his discouragement about that day's counseling session. It must have been God's Spirit at work, because one of the other fellows commented, also quite casually, "Hey, Tom, don't worry about it. We've got enough faith for all of us, including you!" Somehow God used the "coincidence" of the two statements to turn on a tiny pilot light in his heart. That in turn ignited a small flame of faith which started to burn brighter. Before that meeting was over, Tom, to use John Wesley's oft-quoted words, "felt his heart strangely warmed." That turned out to be the crucial beginning of a changed life.

Yes, the miracles of resurrection and release continue in people's lives even today, if we will believe Him, and if we will unbind them.

"You intended to harm me,
but God intended it for good
...the saving of many lives."

Genesis 50:20

10

Joseph—
No If Onlys

Outside of our Lord Himself, is there anyone in the Bible who was a true victim and who, by the power of God, became a victor? Someone who really was a victim of the sins of family, the frailty of friends, and of circumstances in general, but who came through as a triumphant victor? There is only one such person who fits this description perfectly, Joseph. Because of this he has often been called the most Christlike man in the Old Testament. As we look at his life, we will discover the secret of bringing victory to those places in our lives that have been victimized.[1]

When Joseph's father, Jacob, the great patriarch of Israel, was dying, he did something which was very common to those days. He had all his children gather around him and, in the order of their birth, named and described the chief characteristics of each one. In this family it was especially important, since they became the founding fathers of the twelve tribes of Israel.

Jacob's description of Joseph, found in Genesis 49:22-26, is extremely relevant to our theme. Using a remarkably beautiful metaphor, he pictures him as a vine. It is so appropriate to his life that we shall follow that symbol throughout this chapter.

Joseph is a fruitful vine,
a fruitful vine near a spring,
whose branches climb over a wall.

Vines *cling*. But they cling in order to *climb*, to climb up and over whatever gets in their way. In Joseph's case, the vine climbed over walls of every imaginable kind. Not once did he ever look back and say "If only," in order to excuse himself from surmounting the wall. Joseph never played the blame game, though he certainly had reason to do so. Joseph would cling in order to believe, to "trust and obey." And because he did this he always managed to climb over the walls which were placed around him. He was an *overcomer*, or perhaps it's better to say, an *overclimber*. Think of the many walls of victimization that Joseph climbed over.

The Wall of a Mixed-up, Dysfunctional Family

Too often we romanticize the life of Joseph, viewing it through rose-colored glasses. If we read Genesis 29–31, 34–35, we discover the background of his family. Although the sociological customs and patterns of 2000 B.C. were drastically different from today, there are remarkable similarities to the patterns of our dysfunctional families. In that day they had polygamy, one man with several wives plus concubines, all at the same time. Today, with our rate of divorce and remarriage, we have what sociologists call "serial monogamy," several spouses but only one at a time! As for concubines and their children, if one considers the rising percentage of children born out of wedlock, many of whom have different fathers than their siblings, we are struck by the parallels. Jacob's family was actually a series of many interrelated families. Jacob's two wives, Leah and Rachel, and their two maidservants gave birth to a total of twelve children by him. Things must have been "cheaper by the dozen" even then! With the mothers, siblings and half-siblings, grandparents and half-grandparents, we see quite an extended, though not very blended, family. As we read the graphic and sometimes gory details, we are confronted by selfishness, conflict, favoritism, jealousy, hatred, revenge, lust, rape, incest, deceit, and even mass murder. It would make a terrific mini-series on TV, perhaps as "The Battling Brady Bunch!"

Years back I used to do marriage and family counseling without even taking notes. Now I have to make complicated graphs! Several times I have had to say to a couple, "I understood whose are his children and her children and your children. But I can't quite place that child." And they explain about the "divorce orphan," the child of a mate by a previous marriage, adopted by one of the present partners, whose former spouse simply went off and abandoned the child.

A few years ago the Sheik of Immam came to the USA for surgery, bringing with him his wives, children, and servants. He rented the entire floor of a nearby hotel to house them. The local newspaper called the entourage his "family," but a *Time* magazine reporter said it was more like a menagerie. If we made a genogram or family chart for Joseph, we would probably call it a menagerie. Or just a plain mess. That kind of dysfunctional family was the first wall which Joseph, the vine, had to climb over, or perhaps we should say, *climb out of*.

Not long ago we received a belated birth announcement together with a picture of the new arrival, a second son. On the back of the picture these words had been written by the mother, "Just wanted you to see the latest addition to that New Tribe Ron and I started six years ago!" Let me explain. She was referring to a phrase Helen and I have used with hundreds of couples we have counseled or who had gone through our Engaged Discovery or Marriage Enrichment Weekends. When both partners came from disturbed, dysfunctional families and expressed concern about the effects on their children, we always threw out this challenge to them, "Just think, God has begun His healing process in your lives. Though you're not all the way there yet, you're on the road to wholeness and restoration. And now He has brought you two together *so that you can start a whole New Tribe for Him*."

Once, after a counseling session which included this admonition, the husband said to me, "I thought you were United Methodist missionaries. It sounds like you are with the New Tribes Mission."

I want to urge you pastors, counselors, and youth ministers, in addition to every possible emphasis upon the Christian family in your preaching and workshops, to add another important aspect to your ministry. In specific times of prayer with damaged individuals and couples, claim the power and authority of the cross and break the links which chain them to the generational sins of their families. The church seems to be running out of people who come from those "wonderful Christian homes" we used to hear so much about. But don't worry, ever since the beginning, "the God of Abraham, Isaac, and Jacob" has specialized in taking broken, messed-up families, and their hurting, mixed-up children, and turning them into miracles, new creations. But what else should we expect out of a God who took the blackest Friday in history and turned it into the brightest Sunday of all, Easter! We dare to call it Good Friday.

Of all people, Joseph could have looked back and said, "If only I had had a different family!" But instead of wasting energy in blaming, he used it for believing. Did you ever notice these amazing verses in Genesis 41:51-52, "Joseph named his firstborn Manasseh ['Forget'] and said, 'It is because God has made me forget all my trouble and all my father's household.' The second son he named Ephraim ['Twice Fruitful'] and said, 'It is because God has made me fruitful in the land of my suffering.' "

The Walls of Injustice and Victimization

This was a wall, *ten walls* really, one for each one of his jealous brothers. Jacob's deathbed remembrance contains these words:

> With bitterness archers attack him;
> they shot at him with hostility. (49:23).

This is a poetic reference to the treatment Joseph received from his angry brothers. The story in all its cruel detail appears in Genesis 37. When Joseph was a teenager, his father sent him on a two-day journey to see how his brothers were faring, as they tended their flocks at Dothan. What happened is famil-

iar to every Sunday School youngster, for it's such a pictur-
esque scene. Joseph, dressed in his ornamental "coat of many
colors," was seen approaching in the distance. His jealous
brothers plotted to kill "the Dreamer," but at Reuben's pleading, decided instead to throw him into an empty cistern.

Years later, when the brothers were confessing the guilt of
their dastardly deed they said, "Surely we are being punished
because of our brother. . . . He pleaded with us for his life, but
we would not listen" (42:21). We can almost hear his terrified
screams echoing back and forth from the cavernous chamber of
death into which they had dropped him. But they ignored his
pleading and nonchalantly ate their lunch. They fully intended
to let him die there, but when a caravan of slave traders came
by on their way to Egypt, they decided to sell him for twenty
pieces of silver, the average price for a male slave in those days.
They then smeared goat's blood on his fancy coat, took it
home and showed it to Jacob, and claimed Joseph had been
killed by a wild animal. They were guilty of cruelty, child abuse
(a teenager in those days was considered to be among the
children), abandonment, intent to kill, and selling a family
member into slavery. Nowadays someone who had been the
object of any one of these would be considered a victim. When
they are all added together, we would apply the whole family of
words to Joseph — victim, victimization, and victimhood. Many
would say he had a *right to hate his brothers, and ought never to
forgive them.*

Andrew Vachss is an attorney who has devoted his life
to protecting children. He has written several graphic novels
with child abuse as the theme. In a recent *Parade* magazine
he had an article entitled, "You Carry the Cure in Your Own
Heart." It is one of the best descriptions of damages resulting from physical, sexual, and emotional abuse I've ever read.
He writes:

> Of all the many forms of child abuse, emotional abuse may be
> the cruelest and longest-lasting of all. (It) is the systematic
> diminishment of another. It may be intentional or subcon-
> scious, or both, but it is always a course of conduct, not a single

event. It is designed to reduce a child's self-concept to the point where the victim considers himself unworthy — unworthy of respect, unworthy of friendship, unworthy of the natural birthright of all children: love and protection.

Vachss says we are dangerously wrong in assuming that its "victims will 'just get over it' when they grow up." Emotional abuse scars the heart and damages the soul. Like cancer it does its most deadly work internally, and like cancer it can metastasize if untreated.

Much of what Vachss writes regarding self-reference and the building of self-esteem is excellent. I fully agree with his emphasis that victims are under no obligation to try to understand or to rehabilitate their abusers. However, there is one particular part of his *prescription* for healing with which I disagree radically. It is his almost violent opposition to forgiving those who have wronged us.

> A particularly pernicious myth is that "healing requires forgiveness" of the abuser . . . a victim handicapped by the need to "forgive" is a handicapped helper indeed. . . . The abuser has no "right" to forgiveness — such blessings can only be earned. And although the damage was done with words, true forgiveness can only be earned with deeds.[2]

This is the common attitude among many secular counselors, who insist on holding onto anger and resentment toward wrongdoers, in order to find inner strength, self-respect, and a new identity. This contains a half-truth — that it is healthy to express our true feelings of anger and pain against those who have hurt us. According to Paul's admonition in Ephesians 4:26-27, this is spiritually healthy. But to carry this anger further, until it becomes maintained resentment, is unhealthy and gives the devil a foothold in our lives. Jesus never gave us any option other than to forgive "those who trespass against us." He continuously insisted that if we do not forgive others their sins against us, God cannot truly forgive us of our sins (Matthew 6:14-15, 18:35; Mark 11:25; Luke 6:37).

Even from a purely medical and psychological viewpoint, the secular counsel is not only incorrect but actually exacerbates the problem. Forgiving our wrongdoers is absolutely fundamental for our own physical and emotional health. This should not surprise us in the least. Since we have been created in the image of God, and designed to function according to His built-in laws, then the *morally right* behavior must always be the *healthy* behavior.

Within the last decade several books, written as the result of careful scientific research, have proved conclusively that retained anger, hostility, and an unforgiving spirit are directly connected to serious heart diseases as well as emotional illnesses. Dr. Redford Williams of the Duke University Medical Center is a leading researcher in this field. As I was reading his book, *The Trusting Heart*,[3] I kept saying to myself, "This sounds familiar. I've read all this before somewhere." Then suddenly I remembered. Dr. Jesus had said it all 2,000 years ago, in His small treatise called the Sermon on the Mount! Yes, God's truth is the same, whether it is the *disclosed* truth of divine *revelation* or the *discovered* truth of human *reason*.

The importance of forgiveness has been fully confirmed by my counseling experience. Abuse victims who do not forgive their abusers, but hold on to their bitterness, never truly become free from them. Everything in their lives consciously and subconsciously revolves around the abusers. As many have said to me, "I found that whatever I was doing — eating, working, playing, even dreaming while asleep — I was always referring back to them. I felt as if I were chained to them. It harmed my health, disturbed my emotions, and interfered with my personal relationships. Not until I forgave them and gave up my desire to get even did I really feel freed from them. Only then was I able to stop blaming and making respectable excuses for my failures, to find some inner peace, and get on with my life by creating constructive relationships."

This is what makes Joseph's forgiving spirit all the more remarkable, for it took place in an age when vengeance and retaliation was considered both a *legal right* and the *morally right thing to do*. Look at Jacob's description of Joseph once more:

With bitterness archers attacked him;
they shot at him with hostility.
But his bow remained steady,
his strong arms stayed limber,
because of the hand of the Mighty One of Jacob,
because of the Shepherd, the Rock of Israel,
because of your father's God who helps you (49:23-25).

Although Joseph was a victim of his brothers' sharp arrows of jealousy and hostility, when he became the Prime Minister of Egypt and had the chance to punish them with his bow of imperial authority, he never shot back. To pull back on a bow and shoot an arrow requires a tightly stiffened arm. It cannot be done if one's "arms stay limber." It's a beautiful way of saying that Joseph did not harden his heart, stiffen his arm, or take things into his own hands to avenge himself. He left all that in the hands "of the Mighty One . . . the Shepherd and Rock of Israel." Joseph, the victim, refused to use his victimization, but forgave his victimizers and became a victor.

Joseph's story highlights the important distinction between *forgiveness* and *reconciliation*. The Bible does not guarantee that if we forgive, reconciliation with the wrongdoer will automatically follow. Many Christians assume this, and they carry false guilt when it doesn't take place. Reconciliation is a two-way street in that it involves the other person who may not be willing to be reconciled. Therefore, forgiveness often has to be a one-way street. We must always be willing for reconciliation, but we should wait for God's timing. There are some instances where it may never take place. In Joseph's case, though he had long since forgiven his brothers, he had to wait for over twenty years before he could be reconciled to them. Sometimes the two can happen together, as in this recent incident reported by *Newsweek* magazine:

TO FORGIVE IS HUMAN TOO

In a culture of victimization and blame, it is rare to witness a public act of forgiveness. That's what happened last week when Chicago's Cardinal Joseph Bernardin revealed his tearful reconciliation with Stephen Cook, the man who in 1993 accused the Cardinal of sexually abusing him in the 1970s. Cook later dropped his $10 million lawsuit, saying his memories were unreliable. Forgiveness, of course, is the core of the Gospel. . . . Yet in this vengeful era, acts of genuine forgiveness are as unusual as the recognition of sin itself. At their two-hour meeting in a Philadelphia seminary, Cook apologized "from the bottom of my soul," but said that he needed to have Bernardin look him in the eye and say he didn't do it. Bernardin obliged. . . . "I think I have grown spiritually as a result of this," said Bernardin. In reconciling, both *ceased to blame – and thus ceased to be victims.* (Emphasis mine).[4]

The Walls of False Accusation and False Promises

Joseph, the vine, had to climb over several other walls of victimization. In Egypt, as the chief servant in the house of Potiphar, Captain of the King's Guard, everything was entrusted into his care. Potiphar's wife was attracted to the "well-built and handsome" young man and began to sexually harass him. Joseph, however, refused her repeated invitations to sleep with her. What happened next proves the truth of William Congreve's words:

Heav'n has no rage, like love to hatred turn'd,
Nor Hell a fury, like a woman scorned.

One day she angrily tore off his coat and, when he ran away, she cried, "Rape!" As a result of her false accusation, Joseph was arrested and thrown into prison. Although it was a special prison where only convicted government officials were kept, it was still a dark and dismal place, one that Joseph described as a "dungeon" (Genesis 40:15). Once again Joseph was a victim. This time was even worse than the last, for then he was an *innocent victim* of the sins of other people. This time he was a *righteous victim,* because he would not sin and refused to betray either God or his master.

Integrity can sometimes be very costly. In 1987, the team from the town of Conyers, Georgia won the State Basketball Tournament. But a few months later, Coach Stroud discovered that one player who was ineligible for the team on the basis of his grades had played for five seconds in the final game, which they had won by 23 points. He told the principal of the school and they both agreed on what had to be done. So they went public with it and returned the trophy. "I've always taught my team members to tell the truth. How could I not do it?" was Stroud's simple answer to those who praised or criticized him. The story was so unusual that it received national attention and was even carried in the *New York Times*.

After Joseph was sent to prison he proved to be a man of such integrity that he was once again promoted. In his autobiography *Born Again*, Charles Colson of Watergate fame tells that when he first entered prison, an old-timer advised him, "Mind your own business, and whatever you do, don't get involved." Colson observed that the inmate was detached from reality and almost schizoid. This made Colson all the more determined to get involved, to listen and love, and to try to help others.

Instead of looking back and "If onlying," Joseph looked around and helped other prisoners. His interpretation of the dream of a fellow prisoner, the king's cupbearer, proved accurate and the official was released. As he was leaving, Joseph pled with him to repay his kindness by putting in a good word for him to Pharaoh. And what happened? Was the cupbearer so filled with gratitude that he went out of his way for Joseph? One sentence in the record shows how Joseph's high hopes were dashed to pieces, "The chief cupbearer . . . did not remember Joseph. He forgot him."

Months passed, then a year, then another. For two more years Joseph suffered as a victim of the thoughtless ingratitude of a selfish man. He was not only an innocent victim and a righteous victim; now he was a *forgotten victim*. This was the third time around; surely Joseph would now become bitter and start to blame:

> If only my brothers hadn't sold me into slavery,
> If only I had gone ahead and slept with Potiphar's wife,
> If only that worthless cupbearer hadn't forgotten me,
> If only GOD WOULD HAVE REMEMBERED ME!

But He didn't say any of those things, particularly the last one. On the contrary, when he was suddenly taken out of prison and confronted with Pharaoh's flattering statement about his ability to interpret dreams, Joseph turned it aside, saying, "I cannot do it, but God will . . ." He never forgot that God had always remembered him, even when others had not.

Because Joseph *never looked back with blame or bitterness*, but *kept looking up with belief in "the Mighty One of Israel,"* he kept not only his faith but also his self-identity, his self-respect, his self-confidence, and his true selfhood. Though he was repeatedly a victim, he never claimed victimization as an excuse and, therefore, never assumed victim identity. He was truly "a fruitful vine . . . whose branches climb over a wall." His identity became that of an *overclimber,* an *overcomer,* a *VICTOR!*

The 50/20 Vision from the Top of the Wall

When a vine finally makes it to the top of the wall, it is amazing how totally different everything looks. Now Joseph has a God's-eye view of his life and all that he has been through. A *vantage* is "a position which affords a broad overall view or perspective" of a place or situation. And even a *victim* sees differently when viewing from the vantage of the top of the wall. From there he can now understand "that in all things God works for the good of those who love Him, who have been called according to His purpose" (Romans 8:28). Now we can all see that even in the most victimizing incidents of Joseph's life God was at work:

• Being sold into slavery took Joseph to Egypt, where later God had time to make a large nation out of the people, as they lived under Egyptian protection.

• Being sold to Potiphar, Captain of the King's Guard, enabled Joseph to become thoroughly Egyptianized, and brought him within one step of Pharaoh himself.

• False arrest and imprisonment, through a spurned wife's unjust accusations, took him to the royal jail where he was to meet Pharaoh's chief servants and interpret their dreams.

• Being forgotten by the ungrateful cupbearer for two whole years led to his being remembered precisely at the right moment, as the only possible interpreter of Pharaoh's dreams. It had taken thirteen terrible years, filled with injustice and victimization. Nothing had been so accidental or incidental, so foolish or evil, that God could not use it for His purposes.

Yes, from the top of the wall we have the vantage of *sight and hindsight* which always gives us 20/20 vision. Our opthalmologists tell us that's the best vision we can have.

But Joseph had even better vision. He combined *sight, foresight,* and *hindsight* into 50/20 vision. In Genesis 50:20, he told his brothers, "You intended to harm me, but God intended it for good to accomplish what is now being done, the saving of many lives." What Joseph said was literally taking place. Because of his plan to conserve food, the lives of the very brothers who intended to kill him were being saved!

I can hear those who consider themselves as victims objecting, "But surely God does not need our tragedies and traumas, or the sins that other people have committed against us, or our own sins, failures, and blunders, in order to work out His plans and purposes." Of course, He doesn't. *But in this fallen and imperfect world, those are just about all the materials He has to work with.* Most of us have not had the opportunity to choose the materials. *Our only choice is what we will do with them, and what we will allow Him to do through them.*

Joseph, the vine, had 50/20 *faith* as he climbed the wall. After he had reached the top he had 50/20 *vision.* From that vantage, the *senseless* made *sense,* the *pain* had *purpose,* the *misery* turned to *ministry.*

A Fruitful Vine

What was Joseph's secret? What can we learn from him that would lead us from blame to belief? From fruitless futility to fruit-bearing faith and service?

Let us take Jacob's words and update them in the light of Jesus' use of the very same metaphor, the vine. Jacob described the most Christlike man in the Old Testament in an incredible prophecy and prefiguration of Christ Himself, especially as He is portrayed in the Gospel of John. For Jesus said, "I am the vine; you are the branches. If a man remains in Me and I in him, he will bear much fruit; apart from Me you can do nothing" (John 15:5). Joseph was a fruitful branch because he was attached to the Living God, the Vine, the source of all the fruits which Joseph displayed; fruits such as faith, forgiveness, faithfulness, and fortitude.

Further, he was fruitful because he was "near a spring." There are scores of biblical references where the life and power of God are compared to a spring or stream of water. Remarkably, once again, Jacob's imagery is one of Christ's great symbols of Himself. To the Samaritan woman at the well, He declared that He was the Living Water of Life. "Indeed, the water I give . . . will become . . . a spring of water welling up to eternal life" (John 4:14). Later, in the temple, He said, "Whoever believes in Me . . . streams of living water will flow from within him" (7:38).

Joseph was a fruitful branch, a climbing, overcoming branch, because he was firmly united to the Vine which drew its life from the Spring and Source of all life.

I think of another fruitful branch, one of the great victim/ victors of Christian history. Fanny Crosby was a victim of blindness who became one of the most prolific and victorious hymn writers of the last century. There is not the slightest whimper of "If only" in her many praise-filled songs, such as "Blessed Assurance." Joseph's stay in prison was a temporary one, but she was the victim of a permanent dungeon of darkness. She too knew the source of her victory, as in these lines from "Pass Me Not, O Gentle Saviour":

Thou the *spring of all my comfort*,
More than life to me,
Whom have I on earth beside Thee?
Whom in heaven but Thee?[5]

The image of the spring in Jacob's description of Joseph also reminds me of Charles Wesley's great hymn, "Jesus, Lover of

My Soul." How appropriately the final stanza could describe
Joseph in the hour of temptation by Potiphar's wife, drawing
upon the Source of his strength;

> Plenteous grace with Thee is found,
> grace to cover all my sin;
> Let the healing *streams* abound,
> make and *keep me pure* within
> Thou of life the *fountain* art,
> freely let me take of Thee;
> *Spring Thou up within my heart,*
> rise to all eternity.[6]

Joseph was truly "a fruitful vine, a fruitful vine near a spring,
whose branches climb over a wall." And it can be the same if
we remain united to the One who is the Source of our life, and
the Spring which supplies our Strength.

Let me share with you the story of a modern Joseph, in this
case a Josephine, in whose life God turned a victim into a
victor. It's the story of a woman with an unusual name.

Never-Let-Your-Guard-Down Bonnie

About five years ago during a weekend seminar, I told the story
of a young woman who had been freed and healed from a
destructive childhood motto which had kept her bound for
many years. The motto was this, "Never let your guard down.
If you do, people will get to know you and they won't like
you." When I use such illustrations I am always careful to
disguise names and places so as to protect the confidentiality
of the persons involved. But somehow, that night I slipped up,
and quite unintentionally used her actual first name. I assure
you it wasn't the name I've given her here!

After the service a woman came up to me and said, "I'm
'Never-Let-Your-Guard-Down' Bonnie." I replied, "Well, I'm
so glad that her story helped you." "No, no," she said with a
smile, "You don't understand. *I am that woman. I am Bonnie.*
You don't recognize me, do you?"

Suddenly I realized what I had done. I was utterly mortified and started to offer a lengthy apology. She interrupted and again laughingly assured me she wasn't embarrassed. "Feel free to use me to help others anytime you want. I use you to help people all the time."

Shortly after this Bonnie wrote me a letter and explained her whole story. From her earliest childhood she felt she was "an emotional cripple." She remembered her sisters saying, "Something's the matter with Bonnie. One of these days they're going to have to lock her up." She had such a hateful disposition at home that she was given a small bedroom separate from her sisters, because they couldn't stand to be around her. However, at school, church, and in public, she was an entirely different person. Everyone thought she "had it all together," and was a "good Christian." In her twenties, when she got married, she described herself as "the perfect hypocrite."

Then at age twenty-eight, she and her husband had a life-transforming encounter with Christ. This brought about many wonderful changes in her life and marriage, but the inner walls which kept her from letting people get close to her still remained. Those same walls also kept her husband and children out, and even prevented Jesus from entering many areas of her life. Some time later her husband felt called into the ministry, and so they came to Asbury where he finished both his college and seminary education.

While there a friend persuaded her to attend a Saturday seminar which Helen and I were leading. The theme was, "Putting Away Childish Things." She wrote, "I don't know why I went to your seminar. When I packed lunch for my kids, and left them off at the daycare, I kept wondering why I was spending my rare free day doing this. But it didn't take long to find out."

Bonnie had come from a family where she and her sisters had been physically and sexually abused. As she grew older and resisted the abuse, it then began on another sister. For years she had carried great guilt about that, along with many other things. She wrote:

It was hell. I always thought it was because I didn't belong. I really thought God had made a mistake putting me there. How could God love me and put me in a family like that? Once I tried to tell someone about it, but was laughed at and told to stop telling lies.

Until that morning in your seminar, I didn't even know I had a childhood motto. But when I wrote it down on the paper which was passed out, and answered the questions, it was almost as if someone had filled it out for me. I realized that what I had felt was okay, but I was wrong to hold onto it and let it ruin my life. A little five-year-old girl needed to know it was all right to let her guard down and let Jesus love her tremendously! God did something special for me that morning. I have felt good about myself ever since then. I've been able to open up to my husband and children. My husband thinks I'm terrific and tells me so. People like to be around me and I like to be around me too! My children think Mom is special and can talk openly with me. Best of all, when they came to the place in their lives of wanting to accept Jesus, they came to me for help. *That's so special for me.*

More recently she wrote about the grief she experienced when both her parents died within two weeks.

I made it through in a way that glorified God, who was there helping me. But what would I have done if it had not been for all the people who now cared about me, because I let them get close to me? I am amazed at the peace inside my life, in the midst of death, in the midst of raising teenagers, and in the midst of busy parsonage life. God can do anything but fail! Yours in Christ,
Guard Down Bonnie.

Yes, the Source of all life and strength is still turning victims into victors and showing His glory through them.

The Ultimate Battleground

We began this book at the the grave of Lazarus, beloved brother of Martha and Mary, as they complained. "Lord, *if only* You had been here, our brother would not have died." We heard His challenge to the sisters, "Did I not tell you that if you believed you would see the glory of God." Then we followed our Lord as He led them step by step in their journey from blame to belief. We joined them as they not only *saw* the glory of God as *spectators*, but became *participants* in it by releasing Lazarus from the grave clothes which had bound him.

Finally we looked at Joseph, the only human being in Scripture who, though often victimized, never once looked back with a victim's "If only," but always looked up with a firm belief in "The Mighty One of Israel" and emerged victorious. We have seen that he is the clearest prototype of the One who in His cross and Resurrection is history's greatest Victim and its grandest Victor!

Abraham Lincoln said that the only common ground between good and evil is a battleground. The ultimate power of evil is when humans compound evil by confounding it with good, calling "evil good" (Isaiah 5:20). And the ultimate power of God is when He enables humans to say, "You meant evil against me, but God meant it for good . . . for the saving of many lives" (Genesis 50:20, RSV).

As you look at yourself in the mirror of Scripture, are you a victim or a victor? The choice is yours.

Notes

Chapter 1

1. *Time*, 11 July 1994, 26.
2. Charles J. Sykes, *A Nation of Victims: The Decay of the American Character* (New York: St. Martin's Press, 1993).
3. *Diagnostic and Statistical Manual of Mental Disorders*, American Psychiatric Association, 1994.

   Herbert Kutchins and Stuart Kirk, professors of social work at California Universities, have written *The Selling of DSM*, in which they are highly critical of the philosophy behind DSM.
4. David A. Seamands, *Healing of Memories* (Wheaton, Ill.: Victor Books, 1985), 152–57.

Chapter 2

1. *United Methodist Hymnal*, 500.
2. Pascal, *Pensées*.
3. Handley Moule, source unknown.
4. Frank Cumbers, *Daily Readings from the Works of Leslie Weatherhead* (Nashville: Abingdon Press, 1968), 296.

Chapter 3

1. Marlon Brando with Robert Lindsey, *Brando: Songs My Mother Taught Me* (New York: Random House, 1994). Reviewed in *Parade* magazine, 28 August 1994.
2. C.S. Lewis, *The Screwtape Letters* (New York: Macmillan

Publishing Co., Inc., 1959), 67–68.

3. Ibid., 60–61.

4. Oswald Chambers, *My Utmost for His Highest* (New York: Dodd Mead Co., 1935), March 19 reading.

5. Paul Brand and Philip Yancey, *In His Image.* (Grand Rapids: Zondervan, 1984), 108–63.

6. William Barclay, *The Gospel of John, Vol. 2* (Edinburgh: St. Andrews Press, 1955), 113.

7. Henri Nouwen, *Compassion: A Reflection on the Christian Life* (Garden City, N.Y.: Doubleday, 1982), 24.

Chapter 4

1. *United Methodist Hymnal,* 363.

2. Frank Lake, *Clinical Theology* (London: Darton, Longman and Todd, 1966). I am deeply endebted to Frank Lake for the insights of this section of chapter 4. In his book he considers this theme at great length; see especially pages 24–30, and 1090–1148. I know of no other author who has written so profoundly on this aspect of the cross.

3. From a *National Geographic* advertisement.

Chapter 5

1. Brennan Manning, *The Lion and the Lamb* (Old Tappan, N.J.: Fleming H. Revell Co., 1986), 126.

2. Quoted by Roger F. Hurding, *Restoring the Image* (Greenwood, S.C.: The Attic Press, Inc., 1980), 30.

3. *United Methodist Hymnal,* 591.

Chapter 6

1. Maurice Nesbitt, *Where No Fear Was* (New York: Seabury Press, 1981), 35–49. I am indebted to him for several of the insights in this chapter.

2. Edward FitzGerald, *Rubaiyat of Omar Khayyam.*

Chapter 7

1. Paul Brand and Philip Yancey, *Pain: The Gift Nobody Wants* (New York: Zondervan, 1993), 135, 159.

2. G. Campbell Morgan, *The Great Physician* (London: Marshal, Morgan and Scott Ltd., 1937), 100.
3. M. Scott Peck, *The Road Less Traveled* (New York: Simon and Schuster, 1978), 133.

Chapter 8
1. Francis G. Frangipane, *In the Place of Immunity* (Cedar Rapids, Iowa: Arrow Publications, 1994), 83–85.
2. *Book of Common Prayer* (New York: The Seabury Press, 1979), 58–59.
3. G. Campbell Morgan, *The Great Physician* (London: Marshall, Morgan and Scott Ltd., 1937), 177.
4. ABC TV, "20/20," 9 December 1994.
5. Dietrich Bonhoeffer, *The Cost of Discipleship* (New York: Macmillan Company, 1948), 60–62.
6. *Time*, "The Humongous Fungus," (April 1992), 62.
7. This story was told to me by Dr. John Taylor, former Secretary of the Church Missionary Society, and later Bishop of Winchester.

Chapter 9
1. Gordon MacDonald, "The Small Group Letter," *Discipleship Journal* (March/April 1989), 47.
2. Eugenia Price, *Discoveries Made from Living My Life* (Grand Rapids: Zondervan, 1953), 16.

Chapter 10
1. David A. Seamands, *Living with Your Dreams* (Wheaton, Illinois: Victor Books, 1990). This is a detailed study of the life of Joseph.
2. Andrew Vachss, "You Carry the Cure in Your Own Heart" *Parade*, (18 August 1994), 4–6.
3. Redford Williams, M.D. *The Trusting Heart* (New York: Random House, 1989). See also Williams' *Anger Kills* (New York: Random House, 1994); Robert S. Eliot, *From Stress to Strength* (New York: Bantam Books, 1994). See also several articles in *Psychology Today*, January/February 1989, under

"Heart and Soul," 36–59.
4. *Newsweek,* (18 January 1995), 62.
5. *United Methodist Hymnal,* 351.
6. Ibid., 479.